A Guide for the
HYDROPONIC & SOILLESS
CULTURE GROWER

A Guide for the
HYDROPONIC & SOILLESS
CULTURE GROWER

J. BENTON JONES, JR.

TIMBER PRESS
Portland, Oregon
1983

TIMBER PRESS
P.O. Box 1631
Beaverton, Oregon 97075

Contents

Illustrations

Acknowledgements

The author would like to express his appreciation to James Brown of Hygroponics, Incorporated, of Panama City, Florida: Dr. Harold Stern of the HACH Chemical Company of Ames, Iowa; Barry Piesner, U.S. Agro Systems of Holbrook, New York; and Peter Pelton, Normandy Technologies of St. Louis, Missouri for supplying the photographs used in this book. Special thanks goes to Richard Abel for his constructive suggestions and editorial comments during the preparation of the manuscript.

This book is dedicated to my wife, Judy, for her encouragement and support during the preparation of the manuscript.

Chapter I: Introduction

The growing of plants in water or in a nutrient solution, more recently referred to as HYDROPONICS (the word HYDRO meaning water and the word PONOS meaning labor, i.e. WORKING WATER), has been practiced for centuries. In more recent times, this technique has become of considerable commercial interest for plant production. Widely used as a research technique, the soilless culture of plants was popularized in the 1930s, and many articles and books have been written on the subject in recent years. Actually hydroponics is only one form of soilless culture, referring to a technique in which plant roots are suspended in either a static continuously aerated nutrient solution, or a continuously flowing or a mist of nutrient solution. Plants growing in beds of an inorganic substance, such as sand or gravel, or in an organic material such as, sphagnum peat or pine bark, and periodically watered with a nutrient solution, should be referred to as soilless culture but not necessarily HYDROPONIC. Some may argue with these definitions since the common conception of HYDROPONICS is one in which plants are grown in a gravel or sand bed that is periodically bathed with a nutrient solution.

Most of the books on soilless culture focus on the general culture of plants and the design of the soilless systems, giving sketchy details on the composition and management of the nutrient solution. Although the methods of solution delivery and plant support media may vary considerably between soilless systems, most have proven to be workable, resulting in reasonably good plant growth. However, a working system and one that is commercially successful are quite different. Unfortunately, many workable soilless culture systems are not commercially sound. Most books would lead one to believe that soilless culture is a simple method for plant growing and one relatively free from problems. Experience has shown that soilless growing requires attention to detail and good growing skill. Most soilless growing systems are not easy to manage for the inexperienced and unskilled. Soil growing is more forgiving of errors made by the grower than most soilless culture systems, particularly those that are hydroponic.

Proper instruction in the design and workings of a soilless culture system is absolutely essential. Those who are not familiar with the potential hazards associated with these systems or fail to understand the chemistry of the nutrient solution required for its proper management, will normally fail to achieve commercial success with most soilless culture systems.

This book describes the various systems of soilless growing and those characteristics essential for success. The common procedures for inorganic, organic media, and hydroponic culture are described with emphasis on the essentials of the technique. The reader is advised to seek other sources for general information on plant production.

The use of trade names and particular products in this book does not imply endorsement of the products named or criticism of similar ones not named, but rather as an example for illustration purposes.

Chapter II: How Plants Grow

The ancient men of knowledge wondered about how plants grew, concluding that the plant obtained its nourishment from the soil, calling it a "particular juyce" existent in the soil for plants. In the 16th century, van Helmont regarded water as the sole nutrient for plants. Growing a willow in a large carefully weighed tub of soil, he observed at the end of the experiment that only 2 ounces of soil was lost during the period of the experiment, while the willow increased in weight from 5 to 169 pounds. Since only water was added to the soil, van Helmont concluded that plant growth was produced solely by water.

Later in the 16th century, John Woodward grew spearmint in various kinds of water and observed that growth increased with increasing impurity of the water. He concluded that plant growth increased in water containing increasing amounts of terrestrial matter because this matter is left behind in the plant as water passes through the plant.

The idea that soil water carried "food" for plants and that the plant "lives off the soil," dominated the thinking of the times. It wasn't until the mid and late 18th century that experimenters began to really understand how, indeed, plants did grow.

A book entitled "The Principle of Agriculture and Vegetation" published in 1757 by the Ediburgh Society and written by Francis Home, introduced a number of factors which were believed to be related to plant growth. Further, Home recognized the value of pot experiments and plant analysis as means of determining those factors affecting plant growth. His book attracted considerable attention and led experimenters to explore both the soil and the plant more intensively.

Joseph Priestley's famous experiment in 1775 with an animal and a mint plant enclosed in the same vessel established the fact that plants will purify air rather than deplete the air as do animals. His results opened a whole new area of investigation. Twenty-five years later, DeSaussure determined that plants consume carbon dioxide from the air and release oxygen when in the light. Thus, the process that we today call "photosynthesis" was discovered, although it was not well understood by DeSaussure or others at that time.

At about the same time, and as an extension of earlier observations, the "humus" theory of plant growth was proposed and widely accepted. The concept postulated that plants obtain carbon and essential nutrients from soil humus. This was probably the first suggestion for what we would call today the "organic gardening" concept of plant growth and well being. A number of experiments and observations made by many since then have discounted the basic premise of the "humus theory."

In the middle of the 19th century, an experimenter named Boussingault began to carefully observe plants, measuring their growth and determining their composition as they grew in different types of treated soil. This was the beginning of many experiments that followed, demonstrating that the soil could be manipulated through the additions of manures and other chemicals to affect plant growth and yield. However, these observations did not explain why plants responded to changing soil conditions. Then came another famous report in 1840 by Liebig which stated that plants obtain all their carbon from the carbon dioxide in the air. A new era of understanding about plants and how they grow emerged. For the first time it was understood that plants utilized substances both in the soil and air. Subsequent efforts turned to identifying those substances in soil or added to soil which would optimize plant growth in desired directions.

The value and effect of certain chemicals and manures on plant growth took on new meaning. The field experiments conducted by Lawes and Gilbert at Rothamstad (England) led to the concept that substances other than the soil itself can influence plant growth. About this time, the water experiments by Knop and other plant physiologists showed conclusively that potassium (K), magnesium (Mg), calcium (Ca), iron (Fe), phosphorus (P), along with sulfur (S), carbon (C), nitrogen (N), hydrogen (H) and oxygen (O) are all necessary for plant life. It is interesting to observe that the formula devised by Knop for growing plants in a nutrient solution can still be used successfully today in most hydroponic systems (Table 1).

TABLE 1.   KNOP'S NUTRIENT SOLUTION

Compound	g/l
KNO_3	0.2
$Ca(NO_3)_2$	0.8
KH_2PO_4	0.2
$MgSO_4 \cdot 7H_2O$	0.2
$FePO_4$	0.1

It should be remembered that the mid 19th century was a time of intense scientific discovery. The investigators named above are but a few of those who made significant discoveries that influenced the thinking and course of scientific biological investigation. Many of the major discoveries of their day centered on biological systems, both plant and animal. Before the turn of the 19th century, the scientific basis of plant growth was well established. Research had conclusively proved that plants obtained carbon (C), hydrogen (H) and oxygen (O) required for carbohydrate synthesis from carbon dioxide and water, respectively; that nitrogen (N) was obtained by root absorption of ammonium- and nitrate-ions, [although leguminous plants can supplement with nitrogen (N_2) from the air]; and that all the other elements are taken up from the soil as ions. This general outline remains the basis for the present day understanding of plant growth, although we now know that there are 16 essential elements, and have extended our knowledge about how these elements function in plants, at what levels they are required to maintain healthy and vigorous growth, and how they are absorbed and translocated.

Although there is much that we do know about plants and how they grow, there is still much that we don't know, particularly about the role of essential elements. Balance, that is the relationship of one element to another, may be as important as the concentration of any one of the elements in optimizing plant nutrition. There is still considerable uncertainty as to how elements are absorbed by the plant roots and then how they move within the plant. Elemental form, whether individual ions or complexes, may be as important for movement and utilization as concentration. For example, chelated iron (Fe) forms are effective for Fe deficiency control, although ionic Fe, either as the ferric (Fe^{+++}) or ferrous (Fe^{++}) ions, is equally effective but at a lower concentration.

The biologically active portion of an element in the plant, frequently referred to as the LABILE form, may be that portion of the concentration in plants that determines the character of plant growth. The use of TISSUE TESTS (see page 88) is partly based on this concept, measuring that portion of the element that is found in the plant sap and then relating this concentration to plant growth.

Plant nutrition is attracting considerable attention today as plant physiologists and soil fertility specialists attempt to answer questions about how plants utilize the essential elements. As our understanding advances, this knowledge can be put into practice, making all forms of growing, hydroponic or otherwise, more productive.

Figure 1. Solution culture set-up used by Sachs in the middle of the nineteenth century. The roots are immersed in the nutrient solution. From Julius von Sachs, *Lectures on the Physiology of Plants*, Clarendon Press, Oxford, 1887.

Chapter III: Soil and Hydroponics

Scientifically speaking, plant growth in all rooting media, including soil, is HYDROPO-NIC, since the elements absorbed by plant roots must be in a water based solution. The concentration and movement of the elements within this solution depends on the nature of the surrounding medium. For example, in soil, the soil solution and its elemental composition are the result of many interacting factors, an ever changing dynamic system of complex equilibrium chemistry in which the soil, soil microorganisms and the plant root each play unique and specific roles which alter the AVAILABILITY and eventual absorption by the plant root of the elements required for growth. The complexity of the chemistry of the soil (nutrient) solution is significantly simplified when the support media is inert, as in sand or gravel culture, and becomes even simpler when the plant roots are suspended in a nutrient solution, as in the case of the Nutrient Film Technique (NFT) method of growing.

There are those who consider soil growing as a system that is "out of control," while hydroponics is classed as a system for control. This would seem at first glance to be a reasonable assessment, although not entirely true in practice. A soil system is indeed difficult to keep in control due to the complex inorganic-organic and biological nature of soil. Plants growing in soil are frequently competitors for the essential elements in the soil solution. This competition is essentially eliminated in a hydroponic system. Therefore, the grower has the ability to REGULATE the composition of the nutrient solution and in turn, control to a considerable degree plant growth. The challenge for the hydroponic grower is the control of the nutrient solution composition, a topic dealt with in some detail in this book.

Those holding the ORGANIC view of plant growth and development have considerable difficulty in accepting hydroponics as a NATURAL system of plant production. Their contention is that unless the elements essential for plants are derived from an ORGANIC or NATURAL source, plant growth and development are deficient, and therefore UNNATU-RAL. Scientific proof, that such is the case is lacking, although many argue the NATURAL point of view with considerable elegance, despite the want of factual substantiation.

A case may be made about PURITY which has some degree of scientific validity. For example, it has been demonstrated that in carefully controlled environments, laboratory mice frequently do not do as well when placed into a PURE environment (that is, free from substances thought to be harmful and/or not needed) as compared to those exposed to typical dirty environments. These experiments suggest that man does not know all there is to know about the growth and well being of laboratory mice, and probably less about plants. This observation may have some degree of significance when dealing with a soilless system of plant culture in choosing the source of the chemicals, support media and water that are to be used. Within certain limits, a less pure system may be more desirable than one which uses purified ingredients.

This poses an interesting problem for the soilless culture grower when designing his growing system. Pure chemicals (analytical or technical grades) used for making the nutrient solution, purified water; and either no support media or an inert one may not be the best of alternatives. Plant growth, and probably yield, may be considerably better in a soilless culture system that exposes the plant to a more natural environment than one which is "laboratory" sterile. This may also explain the observation that in some instances the ORGANIC system benefits from the complexities of the natural environment as compared to a system constituted and controlled by man on the basis of current scientific knowledge.

It was early recognized by those utilizing the solution culture system that more than the major and micro essential elements were needed to achieve maximum growth. To ensure that ALL of the elements that might favorably affect plant growth are present in the nutrient solution, an A-Z micronutrient solution was recommended as given in Table 7 (see page 72). Included in the two part solution are 20 elements:

Aluminium (Al)	Cadmium (Cd)	Lead (Pb)	Selenium (Se)
Arsenic (As)	Cobalt (Co)	Lithium (Li)	Strontium (Sr)
Barium (Ba)	Chromium (Cr)	Mercury (Hg)	Tin (Sn)
Bismuth (Bi)	Fluorine (F)	Nickel (Ni)	Titanium (Ti)
Bromine (Br)	Iodine (I)	Rubidium (Rb)	Vanadium (V)

These elements are not currently considered essential but are found in plants and the natural environment, generally at trace concentrations. Eight of these elements are recognized as essential for animals, plus 2 that are possibly essential. The A-Z micronutrient solution is little used although it does point to the possibility that most, if not all of these elements, can be beneficial to plant growth and deserve some attention. The so-called BENEFICIAL ELEMENTS will be discussed in greater detail in Chapter V.

Therefore, for the soilless media and hydroponic grower, the attempt is to duplicate, in part, the role soil plays in supplying and controlling essential element availability. In some ways, this task is easier, and in others, more difficult when it must be done almost entirely by means of a chemically made nutrient solution.

In soil, elemental uptake is affected by the movement of the elements in the soil solution and by the growth of plant roots. Elements move with soil water. This movement, called MASS FLOW, carries elements to and away from plant roots. Within the soil solution itself, elements move from regions of high to low concentrations by DIFFUSION. Thus, as elements are absorbed by plant roots, a concentration gradient is formed which provides a mechanism for resupply. The plant also plays a role by ROOT EXTENSION (growth) into the soil mass, bringing greater contact between the root surfaces and soil.

Much of this complexity of the root-soil phenomena is reduced in soilless media and hydroponic systems, where the plant roots are periodically bathed with a moving nutrient solution which contains most of the essential elements required by the plant. The application of the nutrient solution acts much like MASS FLOW behavior in soil systems. The role of DIFFUSION and ROOT EXTENSION is reduced in these non-soil systems.

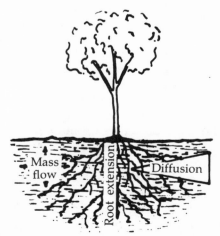

Figure 2. The elements dissolved in the soil water are carried through the soil by MASS FLOW and elements within the soil solution move from areas of high concentration to low by DIFFUSION. The plant increases its contact with the soil and water surrounding soil particles by growing and extending roots into the soil mass by ROOT EXTENSION. These processes either bring the plant roots in contact with more elements or carry away elements from potential contact with roots.

Chapter IV: The Essential Elements

Through the years a set of terms has been developed to classify those elements which are essential for plant growth. This terminology can be confusing and misleading to those unfamiliar with it. Even the experienced become rattled from time to time.

As with any body of knowledge, a jargon develops which is accepted but only understood well by those actively engaged in the field. One of the commonly misused terms is MINERAL, when referring to the essential metallic elements, such as copper (Cu), iron (Fe), zinc (Zn), etc. The strict definition of mineral refers to a compound of elements and not a single element. But one hears of MINERAL NUTRITION when referring to plant elemental nutrition. This phrase occasionally appears in conjunction with other words, such as PLANT MINERAL NUTRITION or PLANT NUTRITION—all referring to the essential elements and their influence on plants.

Another commonly misused and misunderstood word is NUTRIENT, referring again to an essential element. It is becoming increasingly common to combine the words, NUTRIENT and ELEMENT, to mean an essential element. Therefore, elements like nitrogen (N), phosphorus (P), potassium (K), etc., are called NUTRIENT ELEMENTS. Unfortunately, no one has suggested what is the proper terminology when taking about the essential elements, so the literature on plant nutrition contains a mixture of these words to describe the same thing. In this book ESSENTIAL ELEMENT or ELEMENT will be used in place of NUTRIENT ELEMENT or NUTRIENT.

The early plant investigators developed a set of terms to classify the essential elements. The MAJOR elements* include nitrogen (N), phosphorus (P) and potassium (K), since they are found in sizeable quantities in plant tissues. Those elements found in smaller quantities were at first called MINOR ELEMENTS or sometimes TRACE ELEMENTS. These elements are boron (B), chlorine (Cl), copper (Cu), iron (Fe), manganese (Mn), molybdenum (Mo) and zinc (Zn). More recently, these elements have been renamed the MICRONU-TRIENTS, a term which better fits the comparative ratios between the MAJOR elements found in sizeable concentrations, and the MICRONUTRIENTS, found at lower concentrations in plant tissues. Unfortunately, however, three of the essential elements, calcium (Ca), magnesium (Mg) and sulfur (S) were named SECONDARY ELEMENTS. The so-called SECONDARY ELEMENTS should be considered as MAJOR ELEMENTS and are so referred to in this text. These changes in terminology are helpful in removing the connotation that being either a MAJOR or MICRONUTRIENT ELEMENT indicates their degree of significance as an essential element, when nothing could be farther from the truth.

Another catagory has begun to make its way into the plant nutrition literature, the so-called BENEFICIAL ELEMENTS. Discussion of these elements will be deferred for consideration later (Chapter V).

The word AVAILABLE has developed a specific connotation in plant nutrition parlance. It refers to that form of the element that can be absorbed by the plant. Although its use has been more closely allied with soil growing, it has inappropriately appeared in the hydroponic literature. An element to be taken into the plant must be in a soluble form in the water solution surrounding the roots. The AVAILABLE form for most elements in solution is as an ion. It should be pointed out, however, that some molecular forms of the elements can also be absorbed. For example, the molecule urea (a soluble form of nitrogen) as well as some chelated complexes (such as FeEDTA) can be absorbed by the plant root. Consideration of elemental form will be discussed in more detail later.

---

* Carbon (C), hydrogen (H) and oxygen (O) are also MAJOR ELEMENTS but are not normally thought of in the context of those elements primarily absorbed by plants through the roots.

The criteria for ESSENTIALITY were established by two University of California plant physiologists in a paper published in 1939[1]. Arnon and Stout described three requirements that an element had to meet to be considered ESSENTIAL for plants:

1. Omission of the element in question must result in abnormal growth, failure to complete the life cycle, or premature death of the plant;
2. The element must be specific and not replaceable by another; and
3. The element must exert its effect directly on growth or metabolism and not by some indirect effect, such as by antagonizing another element present at a toxic level.

Some plant physiologists feel that the criteria established by Arnon and Stout may have inadvertently fixed the number of ESSENTIAL elements at the current 16 and that for the foreseeable future no additional elements will be found which will meet these criteria for essentiality. A list of the 16 ESSENTIAL elements, the form utilized and their biochemical function in plants, is given in Table 2.

TABLE. 2 LIST OF ESSENTIAL ELEMENTS FOR PLANTS BY FORM UTILIZED AND BIOCHEMICAL FUNCTION

Essential elements	Form utilized	Biochemical function in plants
C, H, O, N, S	in the form of CO_2, HCO_3^-, H_2O, O_2, NO_3^-, NH_4^+, N_2, SO_4^{2-}, SO_2. The ions from the soil solution, the gases from the atmosphere.	Major constituent of organic material. Essential elements of atomic groups which are involved in enzymic processes. Assimilation by oxidation-reduction reactions.
P, B	in the form of phosphates, boric acid or borate from the soil solution.	Esterification with native alcohol groups in plants. The phosphate esters are involved in energy transfer reactions.
K, Mg, Ca, Mn, Cl	in the form of ions from the soil solution.	Non-specific functions establishing osmotic potentials. More specific reactions by which the conformation of the enzyme protein is brought into optimum status (enzyme activation). Bridging of reaction partners. Balancing indiffusible and diffusible anions.
Fe, Cu, Zn, Mo	in the form of ions or chelates from the soil solution.	Present predominantly in a chelated form incorporated in prosthetic groups. Enable electron transport by valency change.

1. D.I. Arnon and P.R. Stout. 1939. The Essentiality of Certain Elements in Minute Quantity for Plants with Special Reference to Copper. PLANT PHYSIOLOGY 14: 371.

In the case of higher animals, 25 elements have been recognized as essential, with only boron (B) of the 16 plant ESSENTIAL elements not required by animals. The nine elements required by animals but not plants are: arsenic (As), chromium (Cr), cobalt (Co), fluorine (F), iodine (I), nickel (Ni), selenium (Se), silicon (Si) and vanadium (V). A listing of the elements ESSENTIAL for both plants and animals is given in Table 3 and their position in the Periodic Table shown in Figure 3.

TABLE 3. ESSENTIAL ELEMENTS FOR PLANTS AND ANIMALS

Life form	Major elements	Micronutrients
Plants and animals	Calcium Carbon Hydrogen Magnesium Nitrogen Oxygen Phosphorus Potassium Sulfur	Chlorine Copper Iron Manganese Molybdenum Zinc
Plants only		Boron
Animals only	Sodium	Arsenic Chromium Cobalt Fluorine Iodine Nickel Selenium Vanadium

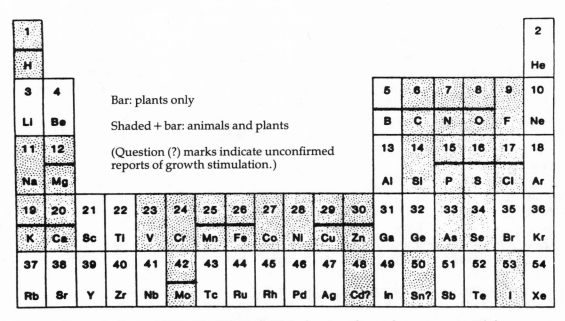

Figure 3. Part of THE PERIODIC TABLE showing those elements essential for plants and animals.

Some plant physiologists feel that it is only a matter of time before the essentiality of cobalt (Co), silicon (Si), and vanadium (V) will be added to the current list of 16 ESSENTIAL plant elements and would recommend that these elements be added to the rooting medium to insure best plant growth. A more detailed discussion about these elements and others classified as BENEFICIAL ELEMENTS can be found in Chapter V.

A. THE MAJOR ELEMENTS

Nine of the 16 essential elements are classified as MAJOR ELEMENTS, carbon (C), hydrogen (H), oxygen (O), nitrogen (N), phosphorus (P), potassium (K), calcium (Ca), magnesium (Mg) and sulfur (S). Since the first 3 are obtained from carbon dioxide and water, they are not normally discussed in any detail as unique to soilless growing systems. However, these 3 elements represent about 90–95% of the dry weight of plants, and are indeed major constituents of plants. The remaining 6 major elements are more important to the soilless culture grower since they must be present in or added to the rooting environment in sufficient quantity and in proper balance to meet the crop requirement. Most of the remaining 5–10% of the dry weight of plants is made up of these 6 elements.

1. NITROGEN (N)

Nitrogen (N) is one of the major essential elements required by plants in a fairly large quantity. The N leaf content of normal plants will vary from a low of 2–3% of the dry matter up to 4–5%, depending primarily on plant species. The N requirement of plants as a percentage of dry weight is highest during the early stages of growth, decreasing with age. However, the total N requirement will increase substantially up to the reproductive stage of growth and then decline sharply.

Nitrogen is a major constituent of amino acids and proteins which play essential roles in plant growth and development. Of all the essential elements, N probably has a greater total influence on plant growth than most of the other essential elements, as its deficiency or excess markedly affects plant growth and fruit yield.

Nitrogen deficiency appears as a lightening of the normal green color associated with a healthy appearance. Since N is a mobile element in the plant, the first symptoms of N deficiency appear in the older leaves which become light green and as the deficiency intensifies turn yellow and eventually die. Deficiency symptoms may develop quickly but can be as quickly corrected by adding some form of available N to the growing medium at a concentration sufficient for normal plant growth and development to resume. Periods of inadequate N may have considerable affect on growth, appearance and final yield, being particularly severe on the plant if occurring during critical stages of growth. Deficiency is best confirmed by means of a plant analysis for total N or by tissue tests for nitrate (see pages 88–92).

There is as much danger in N excess as deficiency, particularly for fruiting crops. Excess N produces lush plants with dark green foilage. Such plants are quite susceptible to disease and insect attack and have greater sensitivity to changing growing conditions. Excess N in fruiting crops not only impairs blossom set and fruit development, but also reduces fruit quality. Excess N frequently does more permanent damage to the plant than does N deficiency.

In most soilless culture systems, proper control of N relates both to concentration and form of the element in the nutrient solution. Most nutrient solution formulas call for a balance between the two common ionic forms of N, nitrate (NO_3^-) and ammonium (NH_4^+), which in turn provides some degree of pH control.

Experience has shown that the percentage of ammonium-ions in the nutrient solution should not exceed 50% of the total N concentration, with the better ratio being 75% nitrate- to 25% ammonium-ions. If ammonium is the major source of N in the nutrient solution, ammonium toxicity can result. However, some ammonium is desirable since experiments have shown that the presence of ammonium in the nutrient solution stimulates the uptake of nitrate. It has been shown that as little as 5% of the total N in solution is ammonium in a flowing nutrient solution system is sufficient. A higher percentage will be needed for aerated standing nutrient solution systems, up to 25% of the total N being ammonium in order to obtain the same stimulating effect on nitrate uptake. There may be required variations of these suggested percentages depending on plant species, stage of plant growth, nutrient solution flow rate, etc.

It has recently been observed that the N concentration in the nutrient solution can influence the character of root growth. As the nitrate concentration increases, the number and length of root hairs decreases. Concentrations of the other major elements, P, K, Ca and Mg, have no similar effect. Even a change in the ammonium content of the nutrient solution has no affect on root hairs. However, roots exposed to high concentrations of ammonium or nutrient solutions with the major source of N being ammonium, will have courser looking roots, with little branching or fine root structure. Root growth and its influence on plant growth will be discussed in more detail in Chapter VI.

Ammonium toxicity results in slowed growth and development. Lesions develop on the stems and leaves, and leaves develop a cupping appearance. The vascular tissue then begins to deteriorate, causing the plants to wilt on high atmospheric demand days and eventually die. If the stem of the affected plant is cut through just above the root line, a darkened ring of decayed vascular tissue is usually clearly visible. Some diseases produce the same symptoms, therefore, careful examination and testing may be needed to determine if an organism is present in the tissue in order to confirm that ammonium toxicity is indeed the cause.

Most formulas call for the total N concentration in the nutrient solution to range from 100–200 ppm, keeping the ratio of nitrate- to ammonium-ions at the desired ratio of about 3 or 4 to 1. The common sources for nitrate-N are calcium nitrate [$Ca(NO_3)_2$], potassium nitrate (KNO_3) and nitric acid (HNO_3); for ammonium and nitrate, ammonium nitrate (NH_4NO_3); and ammonium only, ammonium sulfate [$(NH_4)_2SO_4$], and ammonium mono or di-hydrogen phosphate [$(NH_4)_2HPO_4$ and $NH_4H_2PO_4$, respectively].

Some instructions call for the total N concentration in the nutrient solution to start at a lower level which is increased as the growing crop matures. This is a common practice in the case of fruiting crops when control of the N supply is directed to minimize excessive vegetative growth and to promote fruit initiation and development.

Since N is a key essential element affecting plant growth and quality, either in excess or shortage, careful control of its supply to the plant is extremely important. In soilless growing systems success or failure hinges to a considerable degree how well this element is managed.

2. PHOSPHORUS (P)

Phosphorus (P) is a major essential element, its content in plants ranging from 0.20–0.50% of the dry matter. The P concentration in young plants is frequently quite high, slowly declining with plant age; although like N, total P uptake increases up to the period of fruit set and then drops off sharply. Biochemically, P plays a key role in the plant's energy transfer system, so P deficiency slows growth considerably.

The first symptom of P deficiency is slowed growth and as the deficiency intensifies, the older leaves develop a deep purple coloring. Remember that similar discoloration can also be brought on by cool temperatures, either in the rooting media or surrounding atmosphere. Since P uptake by plants is somewhat temperature affected, a moderate P deficiency may be induced by cool temperatures and corrected by bringing temperatures up to the normal range. Phosphorus deficiency can be easily detected by means of a plant analysis, deficiency occurring when the leaf concentration is less than 0.20% in most plants.

Phosphorus excess was not, until recently, thought to be a common problem. However, several current studies have found excess P occurs easily and will significantly affect plant growth. There is accumulating evidence that if the P content of the plant exceeds 1.00% of its dry weight, P toxicity will result. Phosphorus toxicity is most likely an indirect effect in as much as it affects the normal functions of other elements, such as iron (Fe), manganese (Mn) and zinc (Zn), the interference with Zn being the most likely to occur first.

The likelihood of P excess seems to be a problem more closely associated with soilless culture than growing in soil, although any form of container growing is subject to the hazard of P over-fertilization. In some types of media culture, an initial application of P fertilizer may be sufficient to satisfy the crop requirement without the need for further additions. Phosphorus over-fertilization occurs most frequently when the grower uses a general purpose fertilizer containing P when the only element(s) needed is one (or two) of the other major elements, such as N and/or K.

Most nutrient solution formulas call for 30–50 ppm P in solution, the form of P being either the mono- or di-hydrogen phosphate (HPO_4^{--} or $H_2PO_4^-$, respectively) anions, the dominate anion form being a function of the pH of the nutrient solution. Ammonium and potassium (either mono- or di-hydrogen) phosphate [$(NH_4)_2HPO_4$, $NH_4H_2PO_4$; K_2HPO_4, KH_2PO_4, respectively] are the most common chemicals used to supply P in nutrient solutions. More recently, phosphoric acid (H_3PO_4) has come into increasing use as a possible P source when the addition of either NH_4 or K is not desired.

3. POTASSIUM (K)

Potassium (K) is an essential major element, its content in the plant ranging from 1.25–2.50% of the dry matter. Like N and P, the K concentration in the plant is initially high and declines with age. The uptake of K is substantial during vegetative growth, and after fruiting, declines rapidly. In most fruiting crops, such as tomato, the demand for K by the developing fruit is high. Therefore, plants without adequate K during this critical stage of development will produce fruit of significantly reduced quality. Potassium is mobile in the plant and can move rapidly from the older tissue to the younger, such as developing fruit. Therefore, a K deficiency can quickly result in visual symptoms in the older plant tissue.

It is uncertain what specific role K plays in the plant, although most plant physiologists believe it is essential for maintaining the proper ion balance in the plant. Potassium may also be important for carbohydrate synthesis.

The initial symptom of K deficiency is slowed growth. As the severity of the deficiency increases, the lower leaves will develop a marginal chlorosis. Potassium deficiency symptoms have been described as a leaf SCORCH, the leaves having the appearance of having been "burned" along the edges.

There is a critical balance between the cations K, calcium (Ca) and magnesium (Mg), and when not in balance, plant stress occurs. When K is high in comparison to Ca or Mg, the first likely symptom to occur is a Mg deficiency (see page 21). In some instances, the imbalance can induce a Ca deficiency (see page 21). An imbalance between these three cations is usually the result of excessive K fertilization, K being more readily absorbed and transported in the plant than either Ca or Mg. This antagonism is greater between K and Mg than between K and Ca. Despite these differences, care must be taken to ensure that the proper balance between K, and both Ca and Mg, is maintained in order to ensure that an induced deficiency of either element does not occur.

Most hydroponic formulas call for K concentration in the nutrient solution to be around

200 ppm, the form of K being the K^+ cation. The common chemicals used in these formulas for supplying K are potassium nitrate (KNO_3), potassium sulfate (K_2SO_4) or potassium chloride (KCl).

4. CALCIUM (Ca)

Calcium (Ca) is an essential major element, though frequently and incorrectly referred to as a secondary element. The Ca content in plants ranges considerably from 0.50–2.00% of the dry weight, depending on the plant species. In some species relatively little soluble, or what may be referred to as FREE Ca, is found in plant tissue, with most of the Ca existing as crystals of calcium oxalate, or as precipitates of calcium carbonate and phosphate. It has been suggested that Ca requirement for plants is very low, comparable to that of a micronutrient, with higher concentrations being required to detoxify the presence of other cations.

Calcium uptake rate is less than that for K but remains fairly constant during the life of the plant. The rate of Ca uptake is also dependent on the counter ions in solution, being highest when nitrate is present in the nutrient solution. It is generally believed that Ca uptake is by passive means and that its movement within the plant is by means of the transpiration stream. However, with maturity, Ca movement becomes restricted, and the influx into leaves and developing fruit slows, resulting in potential physiological disorders.

Calcium is a major constituent of cell walls which is probably its major, if not its only significant function in plants.

Calcium deficiency or excess occur in nutrient solutions most commonly as the result of an imbalance with the cations, K^+ and Mg^{++}. In formulas using the ammonium-ion (NH_4^+) as the major source of N, this ion may act like K and become a part of the cation balance. One of the results of ammonium toxicity (see page 19) is the breakdown of the vascular tissue in the main stem of the plant which affects cell wall integrity. This condition is thought to be the result of a Ca deficiency induced by chemical imbalances in the nutrient solution.

Calcium deficiency primarily affects leaf appearance, changing the shape of the leaf and turning the tip brown or black. New, emerging leaves will have a torn appearance as the margins stick together, tearing the leaf along its margins as it expands. Some leaves may never fully expand to normal size and shape when Ca is deficient. One of the major effects of Ca deficiency is blossom-end rot on developing fruit, the result of cellular breakdown at the growing point. Calcium excess is not a common occurrence, although a high Ca concentration may affect the relationship between the major cations, K and Mg (see pages 20,21). Calcium excess may induce either K or Mg deficiency, Mg being the element most likely to be affected first.

The concentration of Ca called for in most nutrient solution formulas is around 200 ppm, the major chemical source being calcium nitrate [$Ca(NO_3)_2$]. Calcium sulfate ($CaSO_4$) can be used only as a supplementary source of Ca due to the low solubility of this chemical form. Also, calcium chloride [$CaCl_2$] may be used to a limited degree at rates designated to keep the chloride (Cl) concentration less than 100 ppm. Calcium exists in the nutrient solution as the divalent cation, Ca^{++}.

Natural waters may contain a substantial quantity of Ca, as much as 100 ppm. Therefore, when preparing a nutrient solution, that quantity of Ca contributed by the water should be determined so that the proper Ca concentration in the nutrient solution is not exceeded.

5. MAGNESIUM (Mg)

Magnesium (Mg) is a major essential element, though frequently and incorrectly referred to as a secondary element. The frequency of Mg deficiency may equal that of N, the result of effects due to improper balance between the other major cations, Ca^{++}, K^+

and NH_4^+. In soil, low pH is frequently a major cause for a Mg deficiency. In addition, some plant species are more sensitive to Mg than others. Magnesium uptake, like Ca, tends to remain fairly constant with time but Mg differs from Ca by being more mobile in the plant. Dry weight of a normal plant will contain from 0.20–0.50% Mg.

Magnesium is a major constituent of the chlorophyll molecule, the substance in which photosynthesis takes place. Magnesium is also an enzyme activator for a number of important energy transfer processes. Therefore, a deficiency will have serious impact on plant growth and development.

Magnesium deficiency symptoms are quite distinct as an interveinal chlorosis, appearing first on the older leaves. Once Mg deficiency occurs, it is very difficult to correct, particularly if the deficiency occurs during the mid-point in the growing season. Some plant species require more Mg than others, the deficiency being triggered by various types of stress. Deficiency can result from an imbalance between K and Mg, or NH_4 and Mg, and possibly one in which Ca may also play a role (see page 21). An interesting side effect of Mg deficiency is a possible increase in susecptibilty to fungus disease infestation.

Under normal conditions, Mg excess is not likely to occur. However, some investigators suggest that the Mg concentrations in the nutrient solution as well as the plant should not exceed that of Ca in order to maintain the proper cation balance for best plant growth and development.

Most hydroponic formulas call for Mg at a concentration around 50 ppm in the nutrient solution, the primary chemical source being magnesium sulfate ($Mg\ SO_47H_2O$). Magnesium is present in the nutrient solution as the divalent cation, Mg^{++}.

Natural waters may contain a substantial quantity of Mg, as much as 50 ppm. Therefore, when preparing a nutrient solution, that quantity of Mg contributed by the water should be determined so that the proper Mg concentration in the nutrient solution is not exceeded.

6. SULFUR (S)

Sulfur (S) is one of the nine major essential elements that has been incorrectly catagorized as a secondary element. Plant concentrations of S range from 0.15–0.50% of the plant dry matter. Some authorities feel that the relationship of S to N is far more important than S concentration alone. Therefore, the N/S ratio would be the better measure of S sufficiency in the plant than total S. Equally important may be the amount of sulfate (SO_4)-S present in the plant, so some physiologists use the ratio of SO_4-S to total S as an indicator of sufficiency for this element. The literature at the present time is confusing as to the best measure of S sufficiency in plants.

Sulfur is a constituent of two amino acids, cystine and thiamine, which play essential roles in the plant. Plants in the LEGUMINOSAE and CRUCIFERAE families have higher requirements for S than most others, since they contain a number of S compounds which are easily recognized by their odor and flavor.

Sulfur deficiency symptoms are similiar to those of N deficiency and can be confusing even to the most expert in plant nutrition evaluation. In general, S deficiency symptoms appear as an over-all loss of color in the plant rather than a loss of color primarily in the older leaves, the symptom typical of N deficiency. It may be necessary, and is probably best, to rely on a plant analysis to confirm a possible S and/or N deficiency problem (see pages 88–92).

Most hydroponic formulas call for about 50 ppm S in the form of the SO_4^{--} anion. The sulfate salts of K, Mg and NH_4 [K_2SO_4, $MgSO_47H_2O$, $(NH_4)_2SO_4$, respectively] are frequently selected as one of the major sources for N, K, or Mg which automatically adds S to the nutrient solution. Little is known about S excess, -whether it can occur and in what form. Evidently plants can tolerate a high concentration of SO_4^{--} anions in a nutrient solution without harm.

B. THE MICRONUTRIENTS

Plants require considerably smaller concentrations of the MICRONUTRIENTS than that of the MAJOR ELEMENTS but they are as critically essential as the major elements. The optimum concentrations for the micronutrients are typically in the range of 1/10,000th of the concentration range required for the major elements (see Table 4). The micronutrients, as a group, are far more critical in terms of their control and management than some of the major elements, particularly in soilless culture systems. In the case of several of the elements, the required range is quite narrow. Departure from this narrow range results in either deficiency or toxicity when below or above the desired concentration range in the rooting media. Deficiency or toxicity symptoms are usually difficult to detect visually and so, commonly require an analysis of the plant for confirmation (see pages 146–150). Deficiency of a micronutrient can usually be easily and quickly corrected, but when dealing with excesses or toxicities, correction is more difficult, if not impossible. If toxicity occurs, the grower may well have to start a new crop. Therefore, great care must be taken to ensure that neither insufficient nor excess concentrations of these elements are introduced into the rooting media either initially or during the growing season.

There may be sufficient concentration of some of the micronutrients in the natural environment, that is in the water used to make a nutrient solution, the inorganic or organic rooting media, or from contact with piping, storage tanks, etc., to preclude the requirement to supply a micronutrient by addition. Therefore, it is best to chemically analyze these constituents to determine their native micronutrient content and to carefully monitor the rooting media and plants to ensure that the micronutrient requirement is being satisfied but not exceeded. Such testing and evaluation procedures are discussed in greater detail in Chapter XI.

TABLE 4. CONCENTRATION OF THE ESSENTIAL ELEMENTS IN PLANT MATERIALS AT LEVELS CONSIDERED ADEQUATE

Element	Chemical symbol	Concentration in dry plant matter (parts per million for micronutrients, % for major elements)	Relative number of atoms with respect to molybdenum
		ppm	
Molybdenum	Mo	0.1	1
Copper	Cu	6	100
Zinc	Zn	20	300
Manganese	Mn	50	1,000
Iron	Fe	100	2,000
Boron	B	20	2,000
Chlorine	Cl	100	3,000
		%	
Sulfur	S	0.1	30,000
Phosphorus	P	0.2	60,000
Magnesium	Mg	0.2	80,000
Calcium	Ca	0.5	125,000
Potassium	K	1.0	250,000
Nitrogen	N	1.5	1,000,000
Oxygen	O	45	30,000,000
Carbon	C	45	40,000,000
Hydrogen	H	6	60,000,000

1. BORON (B)

The sufficiency range for boron is from 10–50 ppm of the dry weight, with the critical value being closer to either the lower or upper concentration of the sufficiency range depending on the plant species. The exact function of B in the plant is not clearly known, although there is considerable evidence that it is important in carbohydrate synthesis and transport.

Plants deficient in B exhibit various symptoms of deficiency, the first being slowed and stunted new growth, followed by a general stunting of the whole plant. Fruit development will be slow or non-existent, depending on the severity of the deficiency. Fruit quality will be impaired when B is inadequately supplied. When the deficiency is severe, the growing tip of both tops and roots will die.

Boron tends to accumulate in the leaf margins so an early symptom of excess B is discoloration and eventual death of the leaf margins. Normally, discoloration along the whole length of the leaf distinguishes B deficiency from Ca deficiency in which just the leaf tip and margin at the tip turn brown and die.

Boron toxicity can easily result from excess B in the nutrient solution or from B found in natural waters. The B level in the plant should be closely monitored by plant analysis (see pages 88–92), and by care in making the nutrient solution and evaluating the quality of water used.

Hydroponic formulas usually call for about 0.3 ppm B in the nutrient solution. The borate (BO_3^{---}) anion is the form found in solution, boric acid (H_3BO_3) being the common chemical source.

2. CHLORINE (Cl)

This micronutrient has only recently (1954) been added to the list of the essential elements required by plants. Relatively little is known about its function, but plants tend to wilt easily when a deficiency exists. The critical concentration range is thought to be between 70–100 ppm in dry matter. Since the chloride (Cl^-) anion is everpresent in the environment, deficiencies are not likely to occur, except under special circumstances. There is far greater danger in excesses of Cl resulting from exposure of plants to salt-affected environments. Symptoms of Cl toxicity include burning of the leaf tips or margins and premature yellowing and loss of leaves.

Chloride is a common contaminate in water and chemicals used to prepare the nutrient solution, so does not normally have to be added. Care should be taken to avoid adding sizeable quantities of Cl to the nutrient solution by using chemicals such as potassium or calcium chloride (KCl and $CaCl_2$). If present in high concentration in the nutrient solution, the Cl^- anion will inhibit the uptake of other anions, particularly nitrate (NO_3^-). Chlorine exists in the nutrient solution as the chloride anion, Cl^-.

3. COPPER (Cu)

Sufficiency of copper (Cu) ranges from 2–20 ppm in the dry matter. Copper possibly plays a role in photosynthesis, as a constituent of a chloroplast protein, and is also known to be an enzyme activator. When deficient, plants are stunted and chlorosis develops on the older leaves. In fruiting crops, Cu deficiency affects the developing fruit, -they are small and imperfectly formed. Death of the growing tip of the fruit may also occur with Cu deficiency.

In hydroponic systems, Cu toxicity can result in significant root damage if the Cu content of the nutrient solution gets too high. The normal concentration range for Cu in nutrient solutions ranges from 0.01 to 0.10 ppm. It has been suggested by some that if the Cu concentration is raised to 4 ppm in NFT systems, some degree of fungus control can be obtained. Additional research is needed to determine if such Cu levels will indeed control common root diseases and not damage plant roots.

Copper sulfate ($CuSO_45H_2O$) is the common chemical source for Cu in nutrient solution formulas. However, there may be sufficient Cu contamination from contact with Cu-containing equipment (pipes, etc.) to supply all that is required in the nutrient solution. Copper exists in the nutrient solution as the cupric cation, Cu^{++}.

4. IRON (Fe)

The essentiality of iron (Fe) has been known for many years and is the most studied element of all the micronutrients. Iron deficiencies are wide spread, affecting many important food crops as well as ornamental plants and trees. The sufficiency range for Fe in most crops is from 25–50 ppm of the dry matter. Iron accumulates in plants without any apparent deleterious effect. Therefore, it is not unusual to find Fe concentrations in excess of many hundreds of parts per million. Total Fe in the plant may be of little importance, being somewhat similar to Ca in that the SOLUBLE or LABILE concentration determines sufficiency. Special tests have been developed to measure this form of Fe in plant tissue (see pages 88–92).

Iron plays a significant role in various energy transfer functions in the plant due to ease of valance change ($Fe^{++} = Fe^{+++} + e^-$). Iron also has the tendency to form chelate complexes. Iron plays an important role in the process of photosynthesis, although its exact role is not clearly known. One of the symptoms of Fe deficiency is a loss of the plant's green color due to the loss of the green pigment, chlorophyll. Although the appearence of Fe deficiency is not too dissimilar to that of Mg, an Fe deficiency symptom first appears in the younger plant tissue, whereas, Mg deficiency symptoms first appear on the older tissue.

Iron deficiency symptoms are not always clearly distinct and can be easily confused with other elemental deficiencies. Deficiencies of S, Mn and Zn frequently produce leaf and plant symptoms that are not easily differentiated visually from those of Fe; therefore, the importance of confirming an Fe deficiency by means of plant analysis (see pages 88–92).

Iron deficiency, once developed, is very difficult to correct. There is gathering evidence that in some instances Fe deficiency may be genetically controlled, with specific individual plants being incapable of normal Fe metabolism, and therefore, unresponsive to correction. Although the use of Fe chelates has markedly improved the control of Fe deficiency problems, deficiency correction is still a major problem in many crops and growing situations. Hydroponically, Fe deficiency control may be easier than in other systems of growing. Soilless culture systems employing an organic rooting media are particularly susceptible to Fe deficiency. This difficulty will be discussed in greater detail later.

Most hydroponic formulas call for the use of a chelated form of Fe to ensure that its presence in the nutrient solution is as an available form. Iron easily complexes with many substances, making Fe concentration maintenance difficult. Since Fe is a common contaminate and found nearly everywhere, Fe may be present in sufficient concentration to prevent deficiency. Normally, Fe concentration must be maintained at about 2–3 ppm in the nutrient solution to prevent deficiency. Iron may exist as either the ferric (Fe^{+++}) or ferrous (Fe^{++}) ion depending on the characteristics of the nutrient solution. Plants can use either ionic form, although that taken in as ferric-Fe must be reduced to the ferrous form. Ferric-Fe can form complexes and precipitates quite easily in the nutrient solution, thereby reducing its concentration and therefore, availability to plants. It is evident that the chemistry of Fe in the nutrient solution and its uptake by plants is quite complex. In addition, utilization of Fe varies among plant species as some have the ability to alter the character of the nutrient solution in the immediate vicinity of their roots, thereby influencing Fe availability. Such influences and their effect on plants will be covered in greater detail later (see page 33).

Although FeEDTA is the most common chemical form for use in nutrient solutions, other Fe compounds are also used. Iron sulfate ($FeSO_47H_2O$) and iron phosphate [$Fe_3(PO_4)_2 8H_2O$] are the two inorganic forms of Fe, while iron citrate and iron tartrate are the two organic types. Of these 4 compounds, iron citrate is probably the most frequently used other than FeEDTA in the more commonly recommended nutrient solution formulas.

As a general rule, it takes about twice the amount of Fe as FeEDTA to provide the same level of availability as Fe in other forms. When using FeEDTA, it is important not to apply more than that recommended since high concentrations can be toxic to plants.

5. MANGANESE (Mn)

Manganese (Mn) is a micronutrient that has a fairly specific range of sufficiency, with concentrations above this range being as detrimental to crop growth as those below. The sufficieny range is from 20–100 ppm of the dry matter for most crops. Plant species sensitive to Mn deficiency are usually equally sensitive to Mn toxicity. The function of Mn in the plant is not too different from that of Fe, being associated wih the oxidation-reduction processes in the photosynthetic electron transport system.

Manganese deficiency symptoms first appear on the younger plant tissue as an interveinal chlorosis. It is not too dissimilar to symptoms of Mg deficiency, except that Mg deficiency first appears on the older plant tissue. In some instances, plants may be Mn deficient and yet give the appearance of normal growth. However, when the deficiency is severe, significant reduction in plant growth can occur. Manganese deficiency can be easily corrected with a foliar application of Mn or by additions of a suitable form of Mn to the rooting media.

Initial Mn excess may produce toxicity symptoms not too dissimilar from deficiency symptoms. With time, symptoms are characterized by brown spots on the older plant tissue sometimes seen as BLACK specks on the stems or fruit. It is not unusual to see typical Fe deficiency symptoms occurring when Mn is in excess. This similarity can result in improper diagnosis which can only be resolved through plant analysis (see pages 88–92).

Hydroponic formulas call for 0.5 ppm Mn in the nutrient solution, the primary chemical source being manganese sulfate ($MnSO_4H_2O$). Since Mn can be easily taken up by plants, care should be exercised to prevent the application of excessive quantities of Mn in the nutrient solution. Manganese exists in the nutrient solution as the manganeous cation, Mn^{++}, although other oxidation states can be present under varying conditions of oxygen supply.

6. MOLYBDENUM (Mo)

Plant molybdenum (Mo) requirement is very low, the critical level being less 0.5 ppm of the dry matter. The Mo concentration found in normally growing plants is less than a part per million, but may be considerably greater with no apparent toxic effect on the plant itself. Molybdenum is an essential component of two major enzymes involved in N metabolism. Nitrogen fixation by symbiotic N fixing bacteria requires Mo, and the reduction of nitrate (NO_3^-)-ion by the enzyme, nitrate reductase, requires Mo. Therefore, plants receiving all of their N by root absorption of the ammonium (NH_4^+) cation, either do not require Mo, or have a reduced requirement for Mo.

Molybdenum deficiency symptoms are unique in some ways, sometimes giving the appearance of N deficiency. Plant growth and flower development are restricted. CRUCIFERAE species are more sensitive to Mo deficiency than other species. WHIPTAIL of cauliflower is probably the most famous of all Mo deficiency problems.

Hydroponic formulas call for 0.05 ppm Mo in the nutrient solution, with ammonium molybdate [$(NH_4)_6Mo_7O_{24}4H_2O$] as the common chemical source. Molybdenum exists in the nutrient solution as the molybdate anion, MoO^-.

7. ZINC (Zn)

Like Fe, zinc (Zn) has been an intensively studied micronutrient since its deficiency is wide spread. Some crops seem more sensitive to Zn than others. The ratio of Zn in the plant to other elements is possibly as important as its concentration alone. The sufficiency range for most crops is from 15–50 ppm of the dry matter. Zinc is unique in that the critical level for Zn in many crops is at 15 ppm. Around 15 ppm, a difference of 1–2 ppm can mean the difference between normal and abnormal growth. Precise measurement of the Zn concentration in the plant when doing a plant analysis determination is critical (see pages 88–92).

Considerable research has been done on the relationships between Zn and P, and Zn and Fe. The results suggest that excessive P concentrations in the plant interfere with

TABLE 5. LIST OF ESSENTIAL ELEMENTS, IONIC FORM IN THE NUTRIENT SOLUTION AND COMMON CHEMICAL SOURCES

Essential element	Ionic form in the nutrient solution	Common chemical sources		
		Name	*Formula*	*Elemental Percent*
Nitrogen (N)	NO_3^-	Ammonium nitrate	NH_4NO_3	N-16 as NO_3
		Calcium nitrate	$Ca(NO_3)_2$	N-15 Ca-19
		Nitric acid	HNO_3	N-15
		Potassium nitrate	KNO_3	N-13 K-36
	NH_4^+	Ammonium nitrate	NH_4NO_3	N-16 as NH_4
		Ammonium phosphate(mono)	$NH_4H_2PO_4$	N-11 P-21
		Ammonium phosphate(di)	$(NH_4)_2HPO_4$	N-18 P-21
		Ammonium sulfate	$(NH_4)_2SO_4$	N-21 S-24
Phosphorus (P)	PO_4^{---}	Ammonium phosphate(mono)	$NH_4H_2PO_4$	P-27 N-12
		Ammonium phosphate(di)	$(NH_4)_2HPO_4$	P-22 N-20
		Potassium phosphate(mono)	KH_2PO_4	P-23 K-30
		Potassium phosphate(di)	K_2HPO_4	K-18 K-22
		Phosphoric Acid	H_3PO_4	P-24
Potassium (K)	K^+	Potassium chloride	KCl	K-50
		Potassium nitrate	KNO_3	K-36 N-13
		Potassium phosphate(mono)	KH_2PO_4	K-30 P-23
		Potassium phosphate(di)	K_2HPO_4	K-22 P-18
		Potassium sulfate	K_2SO_4	K-42 S-17
Calcium (Ca)	Ca^{++}	Calcium chloride	$CaCl_2$	Ca-36
		Calcium nitrate	$Ca(NO_3)_2$	Ca-19 N-15
		Calcium sulfate	$CaSO_4$	Ca-29 S-23
Magnesium (Mg)	Mg^{++}	Magnesium sulfate	$MgSO_4\,7H_2O$	Mg-10 S-14
Sulfur (S)	SO_4^{--}	Ammonium sulfate	$(NH_4)_2SO_4$	S-24 N-21
		Calcium sulfate	$CaSO_4$	S-23 Ca-29
		Magnesium sulfate	$MgSO_4\,7H_2O$	S-14 Mg-10
		Potassium sulfate	K_2SO_4	S-17 K-42
Boron (B)	BO_3^{--}	Boric acid	H_3BO_3	B-16
Copper (Cu)	Cu^{++}	Copper sulfate	$CuSO_4\,5H_2O$	Cu-25
Iron (Fe)	Fe^{+++}	Iron Chelate	FeEDTA	Fe-6 to 12
		Iron citrate		
		Iron tartrate		
Manganese (Mn)	Mn^{++}	Manganese sulfate	$MnSO_4 \cdot H_2O$	Mn-23
Molybdenum (Mo)	MoO^-	Ammonium molybdate	$(NH_4)_6Mo_7O_{23}4H_2O$	Mo-8
Zinc (Zn)	Zn^{++}	Zinc sulfate	$ZnSO_4\,7H_2O$	Zn-22

normal Zn function, while high Zn concentrations interfere with Fe usage, and possibly vice versa.

Zinc is an enzyme activator, involved in the same enzymatic functions as Mn and Mg. Only carbonic anhydrase has been found to be specifically activated by Zn. While Zn probably performs additional roles, they are poorly understood.

Zinc deficiency symptoms appear as a chlorosis in the interveinal areas of new leaves, producing a banding appearance on some plant leaves. In fruit and nut trees, rosetting occurs at the branch terminals with considerable die-back. Plant and leaf growth become stunted and when the deficiency is severe, leaves die and fall off. Moderate Zn deficiency symptoms may be confused with symptoms caused by deficiencies of Mg, Fe and Mn. Plant analysis is required to determine which element is deficient (see pages 88–92).

Many species tolerate fairly high levels of Zn in their tissues without untoward consequences. These species may contain Zn at concentrations in excess of several hundred parts per million without noticeable detrimental effect. However, for those species which are sensitive to both Fe and Zn, such high levels of Zn may induce Fe deficiency.

Hydroponic formulas call for Zn to be at 0.05 ppm in the nutrient solution. Zinc sulfate ($ZnSO_4 7H_2O$) is the common chemical source. Zinc exists in the nutrient solution as the divalent cation, Zn^{++}.

A list of the essential elements, their form in solution and common chemical sources for preparing nutrient solutions, is given in Table 5.

Chapter V: The Beneficial Elements

The number of elements presently considered essential for the proper nutrition of the higher plants stands at 16, the last element added to the list being chlorine (C1) in 1954. Some plant physiologists feel that the criteria for essentiality (see page 16) precludes the addition of other elements, as these 16 include most of the elements found in substantial quantities in plants. But, there may be some elements which will yet prove essential despite the fact that they are required at such low levels that it will take considerable sophisticated chemical analysis to uncover them. The question is, "What elements would these likely be and where would be the best place to start?"

It was early recognized that there may be elements that should be included in the nutrient solution that are not considered essential; therefore, the A-Z Micronutrient Solution was developed (see Table 7 and the discussion on page 14). Eight elements

arsenic (As)	iodine (I)
cobalt (Co)	nickel (Ni)
chromium (Cr)	selenium (Se)
fluorine (F)	vanadium (V)

of the 20 elements included in the A-Z Micronutrient Solution are considered essential for animals. Many feel that those elements recognized essential for animals but not currently for plants are good candidates for essentiality in plants. Those who may wish to explore the potential for discovery of additional elements that may prove essential for both animals and plants will find the recent review article by Mertz[2] interesting.

Three elements are currently being studied for their potential essentiality in plants: cobalt (Co), silicon (Si) and vanadium (V). Considerable research has been devoted to each of these elements, and some investigators feel that they are important elements for sound plant growth.

Cobalt is required indirectly by leguminous plants since this element is essential for the rhizobium bacteria that live symbiotically in the roots, fixing atmospheric nitrogen (N_2) and providing the host plant with its major source of N. Without Co, the rhizobium is inactive and the legume plant requires an inorganic source of N [such as nitrate (NO_3^-) and/or ammonium (NH_4^+) ions] from the soil. It is not clear whether the plant itself requires Co to carry out specific biochemical processes. The irony of this relationship between rhizobium bacteria and leguminous plants is that in the absence of inorganic N in the soil, which forces the plant to depend wholly on N fixed by the rhizobium bacteria, the plant will be deficient in N, cease to grow and eventually die if Co is absent.

Silicon has been found to be required to maintain stalk strength in rice and other small grains. In the absence of adequate Si, these grain plants will not grow upright. This tendency to lodge results in significant grain loss in commercial production situations. The problem of lodging has been observed primarily in paddy rice where soil conditions may affect Si availability and uptake.

Recent studies with greenhouse grown tomato and cucumber have shown that without adequate Si, plants are less vigorous and unusually susceptible to fungus disease attack. Best growth is obtained when the nutrient solution contains 100 ppm silicic acid (H_2SiO_3).

Vanadium seems to be capable of substituting for molybdenum (Mo) in the N metabolism of plants, with no independent role clearly established for V.

There is considerable evidence that some nonessential elements can partially replace an essential element, such as sodium (Na) for potassium (K), and vanadium (V) for molybdenum (Mo). Partial substitutions may be quite beneficial to plants in situations

2. Walter Mertz. 1981. The Essential Trace Elements. SCIENCE 213: 1332–1338.

where an essential element is at a marginally sufficient concentration. Despite considerable speculation, it is not known how and why such substitutions take place.

There seem to be elements that are beneficial to plants, but their exact function and optimum concentration level is as yet unknown. This situation presents real problems not only for plant physiologists but also growers using nutrient solutions to supply most of the essential elements for their crops. The absence or low level of one or more of these elements in the nutrient solution could have marked affects on plant growth and development. There is gathering evidence that a number of elements beyond the three described may be beneficial to plants at low levels, but which are also toxic at higher concentrations. Even elements considered toxic to plants, such as lead (Pb) and platinum (Pt), have been found to have a stimulating affect on plant growth at very low concentrations—between 10 and 100 parts per billion (ppb).

The growing evidence of beneficial effects from elements that are not currently recognized as essential for plants should be sufficient to alert growers that the use of pure chemicals and water for making the nutrient solution may not be the best practice. The presence of small quantities of elemental impurities may well be desirable. Consideration should, therefore, be given to including them in the nutrient solution. Possibly the use of the A-Z Micronutrient Solution should be encouraged again (see Table 7).

Chapter VI: The Root and the Root Environment

Presently, we do not have a clear understanding of how ions move from the solution surrounding the root into the root and how these ions are transported to the upper portions of the plant. It is known that the absorption of ions by the root is both a PASSIVE and ACTIVE process.

PASSIVE root absorption means that an ion is carried into the root by the passage of water, that is, it is sort of CARRIED along in the water taken into the plant. It is believed that the PASSIVE mode of transport explains the high concentrations of some anions, such as nitrate (NO_3^-) and chloride (Cl^-), found in the leaves and stems of some plants. The controlling factors in PASSIVE absorption are the amount of water moving into the plant and the concentration of these anions in this water. But PASSIVE absorption is not the whole story as a process involving chemical selectivity occurs when the solution reaches the outer cells of the root.

The outer cell walls of the root form an effective barrier to the passage of most ions. Water may move into these cells but the ions contained in the water will be left behind in the solution surrounding the root. Also, another phenomenon is at work. Ions will only move from an area of high concentration to lower. However, in the case of root cells, the concentration of most ions in the root is higher than that in the water surrounding the root. Therefore, ions should move from the root into the surrounding water, and indeed, this can and does happen. The question is how do ions move against this concentration gradient?

The answer is by ACTIVE absorption. It is not entirely clear how this works, but several theories have been developed to explain ACTIVE absorption. These theories are based on the nature of cell membranes. Cell membranes function in several ways to control the flow of ions from outside the cell into the cell. It is usual to talk about TRANSPORTING an ion across the cell membrane, and indeed, this may be what does happen. An ion may be complexed with some substance and then carried across (or through) the membrane into the cell against the concentration gradient. For the system to work, a carrier must be present and energy expended. As yet, no one has been able to determine what the carrier or carriers are, or if indeed they exist. However, the carrier concept helps to explain what is observed in the movement of ions into the cell.

Another theory relates to the existent and function of ION PUMPS rather than specific carriers. The two theories are illustrated in Figures 4 and 5, respectively. The energy required to make both of these systems work comes from cellular metabolism—a process called RESPIRATION.

Although we do not have the entire story to exactly explain ACTIVE absorption, there is general agreement that some type of ACTIVE system does in fact exist which regulates the movement of ions into the plant root.

Therefore, there are three things that we do know about ion absorption by roots:

1. The plant is able to take up ions selectively even though the outside concentration and ratio of elements may be quite different than that in the plant,

2. Accumulation of ions by the root does occur across a considerable concentration gradient, and

3. The absorption of ions by the root requires energy that is generated by cell metabolism.

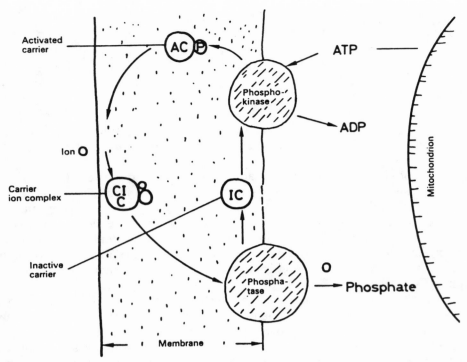

Figure. 4 Carrier ion transport across a membrane involving energy expenditure.

from: K. Mengel and E.A. Kirby 1978 PRINCIPLES OF PLANT NUTRITION International
    Potash Institute, Berne, Switzerland. p 106.

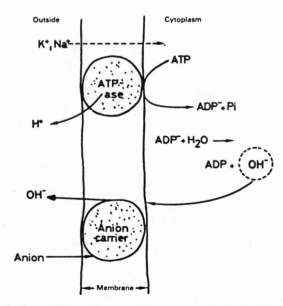

Figure 5. Model of an ATPase driven cation pump coupled with an anion carrier.

from: K. Mengel and E.A. Kirby 1978 PRINCIPLES OF PLANT NUTRITION International
    Potash Institute, Berne, Switzerland. p 109.

A unique feature of the ACTIVE system of ion absorption by plant roots, is that it exhibits ion competition, antagonism and synergism. The competitive effects restrict the absorption of some ions in favor of others. Examples of enhanced uptake relationships include: potassium (K^+) uptake is favored over calcium (Ca^{++}) and magnesium (Mg^{++}) uptake; chloride (Cl^-), sulfate (SO_4^{--}), and phosphate ($H_2PO_4^-$) uptake is stimulated when nitrate (NO_3^-) uptake is strongly depressed. The rate of absorption is also different for various ions. The monovalent ions are more rapidly absorbed by roots than the di- or tri-valent ions.

The uptake of certain ions is also enhanced in ACTIVE uptake. If the nitrate (NO_3^-) ion is the major N source in the surrounding root environment, then there tends to be a balancing effect marked by greater intake of the cations, K^+, Ca^{++} and Mg^{++}. If the ammonium -ion (NH_4^+) is the major source of N, then uptake of the cations, K^+, Ca^{++} and Mg^{++}, is reduced. The presence of NH_4^+ enhances NO_3^- uptake. If Cl^- ions are present in sizable concentration, NO_3^- uptake is reduced.

These effects of ion competition, antagonism and synergism are of considerable importance to all soilless culture growers, and especially so for the hydroponic grower, to avoid the hazard of creating elemental imbalances in the nutrient solution. The nutrient solution must be properly and carefully balanced initially, and then kept in balance during its term of use. Imbalances arising from these ion effects may well frustrate a successful harvest.

Unfortunately, many current systems of nutrient solution management do not effectively provide for the problem of imbalance. Not only is this true of systems in which the nutrient solution is managed on the basis of weekly dumping and reconstitution, but also of constant flow systems. Indeed, the concept of rapid, constant flow, low concentration nutrient solution management is made to look deceptively promising in minimizing the interacting effects of ions in the nutrient solution on absorption and plant nutrition. More about these problems in Chapter VII.

The physical characteristics of the root itself play a major role in elemental uptake. The rooting medium and the elements in the medium will determine to a considerable degree root appearance. For example, root hairs will be almost absent on roots exposed to a high concentration (100 ppm) of NO_3^-. High P will also reduce root hair development, while changing concentrations of the major cations (K, Ca, Mg) have little affect on root hair development.

Oxygen levels and the pore space distribution in the rooting medium affect the development of root hairs also. Aerobic conditions, with equal distribution of water- and air-occupied pore spaces, promotes good root development, including root hairs.

The presence of root hairs markedly increases the surface available for ion absorption, as well as increasing the surface contact between roots and the water film around particles in a soilless medium.

Root size, measured in terms of length and extent of branching, as well as color, are characteristics that are affected by the nature of the rooting environment. Normally, one associates vigorous plant growth with long, white and highly branched roots. It is uncertain whether vigorous top growth is a result of vigorous root growth, or vice versa. Tops tend to grow at the expense of roots with root growth slowing during fruit set. Shoot: root ratios are frequently used to describe the relationship that exists between them, ratios ranging from as low as 0.5 to a high of 15. Root growth is dependent on the supply of carbohydrates from the tops and in turn, the top is dependent on the root for water and essential elements. The loss or restriction of roots will significantly reduce top growth. Therefore, the goal should be to provide and maintain those conditions which promote good root development.

Some plants have the ability of altering the environment immediately around their roots, the most common being a reduction in pH. This phenomenon has been observed in species that have the ability to obtain sufficient iron (Fe) under adverse conditions. This ability may be hampered in hydroponic systems where the pH of the nutrient solution is being constantly adjusted upward or in those systems where the nutrient solution is not recycled. In such cases, care must be taken to ensure that the proper balance and supply of the essential elements are provided since the plant may not have the chance to adjust its rooting environment to suit its particular needs.

Temperature is another important factor which influences root growth, as well as the absorption of water and ions of the essential elements. The optimum root temperature will vary some with plant species, but, in general, root temperatures below 68°F (20°C) begin to bring about changes in root growth and behavior. Below optimum temperatures reduce growth and branching, and lead to courser looking root systems. Absorption of both water and ions are also slowed as the permeability of cell membranes and root kinetics are reduced. Translocation in and out of the root is equally slowed with less than optimum root temperatures. When root temperatures are low, plants will wilt on high atmospheric demand days and elemental deficiencies will appear. Ion absorption of the elements phosphorus (P), iron (Fe) and manganese (Mn) seem to be more affected by low temperature than most of the other essential elements. It should also be remembered that the viscosity of water decreases with decreasing temperature which in turn, affects water movement around and in the plant root.

The maximum root temperature that can be tolerated before significant reduction in root activity occurs is not clearly known. Roots seem to be able to tolerate short periods of high temperature. Roots are fully functional at 86°F (30°C) and probably can withstand temperatures up to 95°F (35°C). However, the current literature is not clear as to the exact limits of the optimum temperature range for best plant growth.

In order to avoid the hazards of either low or high temperatures, the roots and rooting medium should be kept at a temperature between 68° to 86°F (20°–30°C). Reduced growth and other symptoms of poor nutrition will appear if root temperatures are kept at levels below or above this suggested temperature range.

Aeration is another important factor influencing root and plant growth. Oxygen (O_2) is essential for cell growth and activity. If not available in the rooting medium, severe plant injury or death will occur. The energy required for root growth and ion absorption is derived from the process called RESPIRATION which requires O_2. Without adequate O_2 to support respiration, water and ion absorption ceases and roots will quickly die.

If air exchange between the medium and surrounding atmosphere is impaired by over watering, or the pore space is reduced by compaction, O_2 supply is limited, and root growth and function will be adversely affected. As a general rule, if the pore space of a solid medium, such as soil, sand, gravel, or an organic mix containing peat or pine bark, is equally occupied by water and air, sufficient O_2 is present for normal root growth and function.

In hydroponic systems, the grower is faced with a Catch-22 problem in periods of high temperature. The solubility of O_2 in water is quite low (at 75°F about 0.004%), and decreases significantly with increasing temperature. But since plant respiration and therefore O_2 demand increases rapidly with increasing temperature, considerable attention to O_2 supply is required. So, the nutrient solution must be kept well aerated by either bubbling air into the solution or by exposing as much surface of the solution to air by agitation.

All of these factors: root absorption of water and ions; root development and characteristics; the chemical interactions between roots and the nutrient solution; root temperature; and O_2 supply to the roots must be carefully considered and integrated into all soilless media and hydroponic systems. Proponents of various systems neither attend to nor provide information on the best means to manage these factors. The advice provided here is still open to refinement and modification by the practical experience of growers using these systems. But, if growers will control their systems within the ranges suggested, they are not likely to go wrong.

Chapter VII: The Nutrient Solution

Probably no aspect of soilless growing is as poorly understood as the constitution and use of nutrient solutions. Most texts simply provide the reader with a list of nutrient solution formulas, preferred chemical sources, and the necessary techniques for calculating weights and measures. Although such information is surely essential to properly prepare the nutrient solution, a soundly based understanding of the management of the solution is as important, if not more so, for successful growing. The complex interrelationship between composition and use is not understood by many growers, and it is this aspect of nutrient solution management which much of the literature unfortunately provides little or no help. Poor yields, scraggly plants, high water and chemical costs, indeed most of the hallmarks of a less than fully successful growing operation can be directly linked to mismanagement of the nutrient solution. There are, unfortunately, no absolute pat prescriptions or recipes which can be given to growers by any writer. Growers will have to experiment with their own system, observing, testing, and adjusting, until the proper balance between composition and use is achieved in their particular situation and for specific crops.

In addition, the usual management considerations relating to costs for chemicals and water, as well as the energy required to move the nutrient solution, must be integrated into the successful operation of a soilless growing system. One of the major financial decisions involves balancing replenishment schedules against input costs and losses due to single use and dumping.

Although much is not known about how best to manage the nutrient solution, there are many good clues as to what should or should not be done. This chapter is devoted to an explanation of these clues. Growers using these clues will have to develop a scheme of management which best fits their environmental system and crops. They will have to experiment with various techniques to obtain maximum utilization of the nutrient solution while achieving high crop yields of top quality.

Two fairly new terms are now used to describe the two methods of nutrient solution management as either being an OPEN or CLOSED system. An OPEN system is one in which the nutrient solution is used only once in a one-way passage through the rooting medium. In a CLOSED system, the nutrient solution is reused by recirculation. These two means of nutrient solution management pose different problems for the grower which will be discussed in greater detail later.

A. WATER QUALITY

In many parts of the United States, and indeed throughout the world, water quality can be a major problem for soilless culture use due to contamination by various organic and inorganic substances. Even water supplies suitable for domestic and/or agricultural use must be considered suspect by the soilless grower. Since most soilless culture systems require sizeable quantities of relatively pure water, water quality is of utmost importance. The best domestic water supplies commonly contain substances and elements that affect plant growth.

Therefore, a complete analysis of the water to be used for any type of soilless culture system is essential. The analysis should include testing and measuring of organic as well as inorganic components if the water is being taken from a river, shallow well or other surface source. When taken from other than these sources, an inorganic elemental assay will be sufficient to determine elemental composition and concentration.

Natural water supplies usually contain sizeable concentrations of some of the essential elements required by plants, particularly calcium (Ca) and magnesium (Mg). It is not unusual in areas where water is being taken from limestone containing aquifers, for concentrations of Ca and Mg to be as high as 100 and 30 ppm, respectively. Some natural waters contain sizeable concentrations of sodium (Na) and anions, such as sulfate (SO_4^{--}) and chloride (Cl^-). In some areas, boron (B) is found in fairly high concentrations. Sulfide (S^-), primarily as iron sulfide (FeS) which gives the "rotten egg" smell to water, is found in some natural waters.

Surface or pond water may contain disease organisms or algae which pose problems. Algae grows extraordinarily well in most soilless culture systems, plugging pipes and fouling values. Filtering and/or other forms of pretreatment are required to ensure that the water used to prepare the nutrient solution is free from these undesirable organisms, as well as suspended matter.

In most cases, some form of water treatment will be necessary to make and maintain useful solutions. Depending upon what the analysis of the water supply indicates, the grower may at one end of the range simply have to filter out debris. At the other extreme, sophisticated systems dedicated to ion removal by means of ion exchange or reverse osmosis as well as filtering using sand beds or millipore type filters may be required. Between these extreme cases, the average water supply may be used simply by adjusting through the addition of some essential elements knowing that the water being used will supply a portion or all of the remainder required. For example, in HARD WATER areas, there may be sufficient Ca and Mg in the water to provide most or all of the plant requirements, or the micronutrient element concentration could be sufficient to preclude the need to add this group to the nutrient solution. These determinations can and should be made only on the basis of an elemental analysis of the water.

Treatment should be employed only if the chemical and physical composition of the water warrants. Obviously, business, financial and managerial planning must incorporate the costs of developing nutrient pure water in a grower's specified environment. For example, it may be financially prudent to accept some crop loss from the use of impure water rather than attempt to recover the cost of water treatment.

Water samples can be submitted to a testing laboratory, or the grower can do his own analysis using professional kits. The HACH Chemical Company kit is one that can be effectively used by the grower both for water analysis and for monitoring the elemental composition of the nutrient solution (see page 95). The kit is particularly useful if a large number of water and nutrient solution samples are to be checked regularly and the grower has the time and desire to do the work himself.

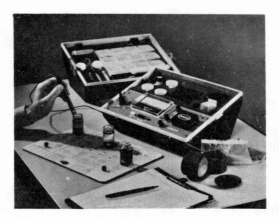

HACH Chemical Company analysis kit for water and nutrient solution assay.

B. NUTRIENT SOLUTION FILTERING

With continuous use in a CLOSED recirculating system, the nutrient solution is altered, not only chemically through the removal of elements by plant root absorption, but also through additions produced by the decay of plant material, the reverse action of plant roots, and the release or development of substances contained in or incident to the support media. As a result, the nutrient solution becomes CLOUDY as suspended precipitates, microorganisms and algae appear.

For short-term use (less than 7 days), the change in the appearance of the nutrient solution is of little consequence. But if the nutrient solution is to be used for an extended period of time and additions of spent elements made to extend its use, then these changes require special attention. Filtering is the way in which this problem is best resolved.

The grower has a number of options in filtering the nutrient solution. Swimming pool type filtering systems are capable of removing suspended particles of 50 microns and larger. Removal of particles below 50 microns requires the installation of a sophisticated filtering system, such as Millipore©[3]. Such a system is capable of removing substances that are microscopic in size (less than 1 micron). Thus, such a system removes not only large contaminants but also a number of disease organisms from the nutrient solution.

Filtering the nutrient solution is not a common practice, nor is it recommended in most of the literature on hydroponics. Most nutrient solution management schemes simply call for dumping the "spent" nutrient solution frequently. If water supplies are limited, nutrient solution re-use may be necessary, making filtering an important procedure to maintain the solution in useable form.

Unfortunately, sophisticated filtering systems are expensive and require close attention to keep in proper operating condition. They also add to the cost of growing plants hydroponically. Therefore, what may be gained by filtering, needs to be evaluated against its added cost. Unfortunately, there is little research or practical information available to adequately evaluate cost versus improvement in plant performance, so the grower must make the analysis in terms of his conditions and conservative assumptions.

Size, type and installation requirements for a filtering system will vary depending upon water volume, frequency of use and quantity of material accumulating in the nutrient solution. Cartridge type filters are recommended since back flushing is not generally possible or practical with most hydroponic systems, and cartridges can be easily removed and exchanged. Filtering devices should be placed in the OUT flow pipe leading to the growing bed from the supply reservoir or container. The courser filter should be placed first in line followed by the finer (see Figure 6).

Figure 6. Flow pattern of nutrient solution from the sump through course and fine filters to the growing bed.

3. Millipore Corporation, Ashby Road, Bedford, MA 01730 USA.

To provide some degree of control over microorganisms (bacteria, etc.), in addition to the use of a Millipore© filter, the nutrient solution can be passed under ultra-violet radiation. UV sterilizer, TAM-104[4], has proved to be effective in reducing microorganism counts when two 16-watt lamps are placed in the path of the nutrient solution flowing at 3 gallons (13.5 liters) per minute, giving a total exposure of 573 joules per square meter per hour.

Neither the use of filtering or ultra-violet radiation to control nutrient solution composition has been adequately evaluated to consider either of them essential practices. However, their advantages are worthy of consideration in situations where long, continuous use of the nutrient solution is the practice.

C. FORMULAS AND THEIR MANAGEMENT

Probably no single aspect of soilless culture is as poorly understood as the constitution of the nutrient solution and its management. While it is true that numerous formulas for preparing the nutrient solution have been published, their proper use relative to the needs of specific plant species has been largely ignored. One book[5] lists 160 different formulas varied by salt types and combinations of nitrogen (N) sources. The formulas devised by Hoagland and Arnon (Table 6) are widely used in modified form. It is common to see the phrase "modified Hoagland's nutrient solution" in the literature, referring to their frequently cited University of California Circular 347[6]. A number of published nutrient solution formulas are given in Table 7.

Although a particular nutrient solution formula may be modified to suit particular requirements for its use, the critical requirements for proper management are either overlooked or not understood. The hydroponic literature is marked by much comment on nutrient solution composition in terms of the concentration of the elements in solution, but is nearly devoid of instructions as to how the nutrient solution is to be used, in such common management terms as the volume per plant, frequency of renewal and replenishment of "spent" elements prior to renewal.

Cooper, developer of the NFT system[7], when discussing these questions, remarked, "there is very little information available on this subject." In an interesting experiment, he obtained maximum tomato plant growth when tomato plants were exposed to 13.3. gallons (60 liters) of nutrient solution per plant per week. Thinking that growth was enhanced by the removal of root exudate due to the large volume of solution available to the plants, he studied the relationship between root container size and nutrient solution flow rate. He found that plant growth was affected principally by the size of the root container and the volume of nutrient solution flowing through the container, not by the removal of root exudates. Cooper concluded that more fundamental research was needed to determine the best volume of nutrient solution and flow characteristics for maximum plant growth. He also observed that, "the tolerance of nutrient supply was found to be very great." This observation seems to be in agreement with Steiner, developer of the Steiner formulas[8] (Table 8), who feels that plants have the ability "to select the ions in the mutual ratio favourable for their growth and development," if they are cultivated in an abundant nutrient flow. Available evidence suggests that an advantage of "flowing" nutrient solution

4. Netiv Halamed-He Industries, POB Haela, Israel.
5. E.J. Hewitt. 1966. Sand and Water Culture Method Used in Study of Plant Nutrition. Technical Communication No. 22 (Revised). Commonwealth Bureau of Horticulture and Plantation Crops, East Malling, Maidstone, Kent, England.
6. D.R. Hoagland and D.I. Arnon. 1950. The Water Culture Method of Growing Plants without Soil. California Agricultural Experiment Station Circular 347.
7. Allen Cooper. 1979. The ABC of NFT. Grower Books, London, England.
8. Abram A. Steiner. 1961. A Universal Method for Preparing Nutrient Solutions of Certain Desired Composition. PLANT & SOIL 15: 134–154.

systems arises from the larger volume of nutrient solution available to the plant, resulting in increased contact with the essential elements and reduction in the concentration of inhibiting substances.

The Hoagland and Arnon[6] contributions provide another example of an imperfectly understood and improperly used system. The source of information for both their nutrient solution formulas was obtained from the determination of the average elemental content of the tomato plant. They calculated the elemental concentration required based on one plant growing in 4 gallons (18 liters) of nutrient solution which was replaced weekly. Naturally, one might ask, "How would these nutrient solution formulas work if tomato is not the crop, the plant to volume of nutrient solution is changed and the replenishment schedule is shorter or longer?"

Surprisingly, some modification in the use of Hoagland and Arnon formulas seems to have little affect on performance, and explains why they are so widely accepted and used. However, significant departure from the plant to nutrient solution volume ratio and replenishment schedule results in either a deficiency or an excess of the essential elements. It is now apparent that if the scheduling of nutrient solution replacement and/or per volume of solution ratio is changed, the nutrient solution formula must be modified to be in accord with the revised practice, i.e., more dilute if the volume per plant ratio and/or frequency of change is increased. It is common practice to use dilutions of these formulas, so one frequently sees the recommendation for "half-strength" Hoagland's solution, particularly for initial use when plants are being germinated, or are in their very early stage of growth and development. Half- or quarter-strength Hoagland's nutrient solution is frequently used for make-up water also.

TABLE 6. HOAGLAND'S NUTRIENT SOLUTION
FORMULAS

Stock solution	to use, ml/1
Solution No. 1	
1 M KH_2PO_4	1.0
1 M KNO_3	5.0
1 M $Ca(NO_3)_2 \cdot 4H_2O$	5.0
1 M $MgSO_4 \cdot 7H_2O$	2.0
Solution No. 2	
1 M $NH_4H_2PO_4$	1.0
1 M KNO_3	6.0
1 M $Ca(NO_3)_2 \cdot 4H_2O$	4.0
1 M $MgSO_4 \cdot 7H_2O$	2.0

Micronutrient stock solution	g/l
H_3BO_3	2.86
$MnCl_2 \cdot 4H_2O$	1.81
$ZnSO_4 \cdot 7H_2O$	0.22
$CuSO_4 \cdot 5H_2O$	0.08
$H_2MoO_4 \cdot H_2O$	0.02

to use: 1 ml/1 nutrient soln.

Iron

For Solution No. 1: 0.5% iron ammonium citrate to
use: 1 ml/1

For Solution No. 2: 0.5% iron chelate
to use: 2 ml/1

The two most common errors made by growers when using the Hoagland and Arnon nutrient solution formulas are to reduce the volume per plant, sometimes to as little as one plant per gallon (4.5 liters) of solution, and then attempt to extend the use of the solution beyond the recommended weekly replacement schedule. The result is elemental imbalance, poor plant growth and eventual elemental deficiencies.

TABLE 7. LIST OF FORMULAS FOR CONSTITUTING NUTRIENT SOLUTIONS

Name	Reagents	g/l (mg/l)		
Knop's Solution[1]	KNO_3	0.2		
	$Ca(NO_3)_2$	0.8		
	KH_2PO_4	0.2		
	$MgSO_4 7H_2O$	0.2		
	$FePO_4$	0.1		
		a	b	c
Crone's Solution (1902, 1904)[1]	KNO_3	1.0	0.75	0.75
	$Ca_3(PO_4)_2$	0.25	0.25	0.25
	$CaSO_4 2H_2O$	0.25	0.25	0.5
	$Fe_3(PO_4)_2 8H_2O$	0.25	0.25	0.25
	$MgSO_4 7H_2O$	0.25	0.25	0.5
Hoagland and Snyder (1933)[1]	KNO_3	0.51		
	$Ca(NO_3)_2$	0.82		
	$MgSO_4 7H_2O$	0.49		
	KH_2PO_4	0.136		
	Ferric tartrate 1 ml./1. of 0.5% solution			
	Micronutrients A-Z solution shown in Section 8.5.0			
Trelease and Trelease (1933)[1]	KNO_3	0.683		
	$(NH_4)_2SO_4$	0.0679		
	KH_2PO_4	0.3468		
	K_2HPO_4	0.01253		
	$CaCl_2$	0.4373		
	$MgSO_4 7H_2O$	0.7478		
	$FeSO_4 7H_2O$	0.00278		

The Original Rothamsted Solutions[1]		a	b	c	Modified Crone's
	KNO_3	1.0	1.0	1.0	1.0
	$MgSO_4 7H_2O$	0.5	0.5	0.5	0.5
	KH_2PO_4	0.45	0.4	0.3	—
	K_2HPO_4	0.0675	0.135	0.27	—
	$CaSO_4 2H_2O$	0.5	0.5	0.5	0.5
	$Ca_3(PO_4)_2$	—	—	—	0.25
	$Fe_3(PO_4)_2 8H_2O$	—	—	—	0.25
	$FeCl_3$	0.04	0.04	0.04	—
	H_3BO_3	0.001	0.001	0.001	0.001
	$MnSO_4 4H_2O$	0.001	0.001	0.001	0.001

Arnon (1938)[1])	KNO_3	0.656		
	$Ca(NO_3)_2$	0.656		
	$NH_4H_2PO_4$	0.115		
	$MgSO_4 7H_2O$	0.49		
	$FeSO_4 7H_2O$ 0.5%			
	Tartaric acid 0.4% 0.6	ml./1.3 × weekly		

Name	Reagents	g/l (mg/l)
	H₃BO₃	2.86 mg.
	MnCl₂ 4H₂O	1.81 mg.
	CuSO₄ 5H₂O	0.08 mg.
	ZnSO₄ 7H₂O	0.22 mg.
	H₂MoO₄(MoO₃ + H₂O)	0.09 mg.
Arnon and Hoagland (1940)[1]	KNO₃	1.02
	Ca(NO₃)₂	0.492
	NH₄H₂PO₄	0.230
	MgSO₄ 7H₂O	0.49
	See: Arnon's Micronutrient Formula	
Shive and Robbins (1942) I.[1]	Ca(NO₃)₂	0.938
	(NH₄)₂SO₄	0.0924
	KH₂PO₄	0.313
	MgSO₄ 7H₂O	0.567
	FeSO₄ 7H₂O	5.5 mg.
	H₃BO₃	0.57 mg.
	MnSO₄ 4H₂O	0.57 mg.
	ZnSO₄ 7H₂O	0.57 mg.
Shive and Robbins (1942) II.[1]	NaNO₃	0.34
	CaCl₂	0.1665
	KH₂PO₄	0.214
	MgSO₄ 7H₂O	0.514
	Iron and micronutrients as in 1.	
Piper (1942)[1]	KNO₃	1.5
	KH₂PO₄	0.5
	NaCl	0.1
	CaSO₄ 2H₂O	0.5
	MgSO₄ 7H₂O	0.5
	Ferric citrate	0.02
	H₃BO₃	0.5 mg.
	Mn (as MnSO₄)	0.5 mg.
	Zn (as ZnSO₄)	0.2 mg.
	Mo (as Na₂MoO₄)	0.1 mg.
	Cu (as CuSO₄)	0.003 mg. upwards
Robbins (1946)[1]	KNO₃	0.408
	Ca(NO₃)₂	0.820
	KH₂PO₄	0.136
	MgSO₄ 7H₂O	0.493
	Fe	0.5 mg.
	B	0.25 mg.
	Mn	0.25 mg.
	Zn	0.25 mg.
	Cu	0.02 mg.
	Mo	0.01 mg.
Kuwait IV[2]	MgSO₄ 7H₂O	0.34
	CaHPO₄	0.13
	Ca(NO₃)₂	2.0
	KNO₃	0.26
	K₂SO₄	0.02
	NaCl	0.15
	HNO₃ (conc)	13.00 mls
	HCl (conc)	20.00 mls

Name	Reagents	g/l (mg/l)
Kuwait IV (D.W.2)[2]	$MgSO_4\,7H_2O$	0.34
	KH_2PO_4	0.13
	$Ca(NO_3)_2$	2.09
	KNO_3	0.16
	K_2SO_4	0.02
	$NaCl$	0.15
	HNO_3 (conc)	13.00 mls.
	HCl (conc)	20.00 mls.
Gravel Culture-Japan[2]	KNO_3	0.81
	$Ca(NO_3)_2$	0.95
	$MgSO_4\,7H_2O$	0.50
	$NH_4H_2PO_4$	0.12
Basic Formula Bengal, India[2]	$NaNO_3$	0.17
	$(NH_4)_2SO_4$	0.08
	$CaSO_4$	0.04
	$CaHPO_4$	0.10
	K_2SO_4	0.11
	$MgSO_4\,7H_2O$	0.07
Rivoira's Formula Sassari, Sicily[2]	$(NH_4)_2HPO_4$	0.20
	$Ca(NO_3)_2$	0.50
	KNO_3	0.20
	$MgSO_4\,7H_2O$	0.10
	$FeEDTA$	5.13 mg.
	$MnSO_4\,H_2O$	0.73
	$ZnSO_4\,7H_2O$	0.06
	$CuSO_4\,5H_2O$	0.06
	H_3BO_3	0.59
Wroclaw Formula Poland[2]	KNO_3	0.6
	$Ca(NO_3)_2$	0.7
	NH_4NO_3	0.1
	$CaHPO_4$	0.5
	$MgSO_4\,5H_2O$	0.25
	$Fe_2(SO_4)_3$	0.12
	H_3BO_3	0.60 mg.
	$MnSO_4\,H_2O$	0.60 mg.
	$ZnSO_4\,7H_2O$	0.06
	$CuSO_4\,5H_2O$	0.30
	$(NH_4)_6Mo_7O_{24}\,4H_2O$	0.06
Volcani Institute Israel[2]	KNO_3	0.45
	NH_4NO_3	0.35
	$MgSO_4\,7H_2O$	0.05
	H_3PO_4	100 mls.
Penningsfield's North African Formula[2]	KNO_3	0.38
	$Ca(NO_3)_2$	0.21
	$NH_4H_2PO_4$	0.04
	KH_2PO_4	0.14
	$MgSO_4\,7H_2O$	0.19
	$Fe_2(SO_4)_3$	0.01
	$Na_2B_4O_7\,10H_2O$	2.5 mg.
	$MnSO_4H_2O$	2.5
	$CuSO_4\,5H_2O$	2.5
	$(NH_4)_6Mo_7O_{24}\,4H_2O$	0.75
	$ZnSO_4\,7H_2O$	0.02

Name	Reagents	g/l (mg/l)
USDA Formula[2] Maryland*	KNO_3	0.52
	$(NH_4)_2SO_4$	0.088
	$CaHPO_4$	0.22
	$MgSO_4 7H_2O$	0.40
	$CaSO_4$	0.43
Ag. Extension Service[2] Florida*	KNO_3	0.36
	$(NH_4)_2SO_4$	0.08
	$CaHPO_4$	0.17
	$MgSO_4 7H_2O$	0.16
	$CaSO_4$	0.90
*Micronutrient Formula[2] for USDA and Ag. Extension Service	$Fe_2(SO_4)_3$	9.5 mg
	$MnSO_4 H_2O$	0.63 mg
	$CuSO_4 5H_2O$	0.29 mg
	$Na_2B_4O_7 10H_2O$	7.2 mg
	$ZnSO_4 7H_2O$	0.29 mg
Micronutrients A-Z[1] A.	$Al_2(SO_4)_8$	0.055
	KI	0.027
	KBr	0.027
	TiO_2	0.055
	$SnCl_2 2H_2O$	0.027
	LiCl	0.027
	$MnCl_2 4H_2O$	0.38
	H_3BO_3	0.61
	$ZnSO_4 7H_2O$	0.055
	$CuSO_4 5H_2O$	0.055
	$NiSO_4 6H_2O$	0.055
	$Co(NO_3)_2 6H_2O$	0.055
B.	As_2O_3	0.0055
	$BaCl_2$	0.027
	$CdCl_2$	0.0055
	$Bi(NO_3)_2$	0.0055
	Rb_2SO_4	0.0055
	K_2CrO_4	0.027
	KF	0.0055
	$PbCl_2$	0.0055
	$HgCl_2$	0.0055
	MoO_3	0.023
	H_2SeO_4	0.0055
	$SrSO_4$	0.027
	VCl_3	0.0055
Arnon's Micronutrient[1] Formula	H_3BO_3	0.48 mg
	$MnSO_4H_2O$	0.25 mg
	$ZnSO_47H_2O$	0.035 mg
	$CuSO_45H_2O$	0.008 mg
	MoO_32H_2O	0.004 mg

Source: 1. E.J. Hewitt. 1966 Sand and Water Culture Methods used in the study of Plant Nutrition. Technical Communication No. 22 (Revised). Commonwealth Agricultural Bureaux, Maidstone, Kent, England.
2. James Sholto Douglas 1976 Advanced Guide to Hydroponics. Drake Publishers, Inc., New York.

TABLE 8. STEINER'S UNIVERSAL METHOD FOR PREPARING NUTRIENT SOLUTIONS

Concept: Steiner raises the question as to whether it is the relative concentration of elements among each other that determines uptake or the absolute amount. He suggests that there must be a minimum concentration below which uptake is no longer possible and above which luxury consumption occurs leading to internal toxicity. However, within this range, there also must be relative relationships that determine uptake and therefore, the composition of the nutrient solution must be in a particular balance to satisfy the plant requirement for essential elements.

Method: Steiner's aim was to determine how a particular nutrient solution could be prepared which satisfies given requirements as to:
  (1) relative cation ratios,
  (2) relative anion ratios,
  (3) total ionic concentration, and
  (4) pH.

Concerning himself with 3 major anions and 3 major cations, Steiner established the equivalent ratio in percent as follows:

$$NO_3^- : H_2PO_4^- : SO_4^{--}$$
$$80 \quad\quad 5 \quad\quad 15$$

$$K^+ : Ca^{++} : Mg^{++}$$
$$80 \quad\quad 10 \quad\quad 10$$

Using 5 different source chemicals and aliquots to establish the desired ratio of ions and not to exceed a total of 30 mg ions / liter, Steiner's formula was:

Chemical	Normality (N)	ml / 10 liters
KH_2PO_4	1	8.22
$Ca(NO_3)_2 4H_2O$	10	1.644
$MgSO_4 7H_2O$	2	8.22
KNO_3	1	115.07
K_2SO_4	1	8.22

Preparing various nutrient solutions with the objective of maintaining the desired ratio of ions and pH, it became evident to Steiner that if the total ionic concentration was raised above 30 mg ions per liter and the pH above 6.5, only a very few combinations were possible inorder to avoid problems due to precipitation.

Result: Steiner's study reveals the possibility of preparing nutrient solutions that have specific ratios of ions to each other, a set total ion concentration and pH. He sets forth an interesting approach to nutrient solution formula development that bears further study for the inclusion of the other essential elements, forms, such as NO_3^- and NH_4-N, and technique for use.

It should be clear to all who adopt a particular nutrient solution formula that the conditions of its use be learned and carefully followed. If changes are made to suit a particular system, then the "modifications" made must be known and followed for the adopting user to be successful.

Appendix C lists 6 different nutrient solution formulas and use recommendations for a range of crops and growing conditions. These were selected to represent current common formulas having wide application.

The species being grown will require modification in the composition and replacement scheduling of the nutrient solution. Some crops are simply more sensitive to particular elements than others. Therefore, one formula will work well for one crop, and poorly for others. Again, and to the growers misfortune, little is known about this aspect of nutrient solution constitution and management. In fairness, it must be noted that the success of the Hoagland and Arnon formulas have been due in part to the generally good results obtained for a wide range of crops and replacement schedules. It bears repeating that plants do well on dilute Hoagland and Arnon nutrient solutions, and that such dilutions are used to control the rate of growth or for those crops with low elemental requirements.

The ratio of the concentration of elements in the nutrient solution has a marked affect on plant absorption, as has been discussed earlier (see Chapter VI). Therefore, concentration ratios are far more important than the absolute concentration of any one element. The proper adjustment of elemental ratios is particularly important in the relationship between the MAJOR elements and the MICRONUTRIENTS, Further, as discussed on page 33, the ratio of cations to anions in the nutrient solution affects elemental uptake as the plant itself tends to maintain an intrinsic ion balance specific to it. The importance of these balances becomes of far greater significance when elements are absorbed differentially from the nutrient solution due both to plant requirements and alterations in the nutrient solution resulting from different uptake. Therefore, the plant roots "see" an entirely different nutrient solution with repeated use until the nutrient solution is renewed and the full compliment of essential elements in their proper ratios are again available. Such a cyclic pattern of changing nutrient solution composition is surely less than ideal for optimum plant growth and development.

Current thinking about hydroponic growing systems calls for the use of a flowing nutrient solution technique in which the composition of the nutrient solution is constantly maintained either by one-way passage of the nutrient solution through the rooting channel (an OPEN system) or in a CLOSED system by continued replenishment of the depleted elements after each use. The objective is to keep the elemental ion concentration in the nutrient solution constant, an approach that closely parallels the elemental ion environment in soil in which the soil solution is resupplied with ions as they are removed by root absorption. Experiments have shown that plants growing in this type of hydroponic system more closely follow the pattern of plant growth and development obtained in soil. A similar effect can be obtained by growing plants in a large volume of agitated nutrient solution, the volume being sufficiently large that its elemental ion composition is not affected by ion absorption by the plant. Naturally, such a system of growing would not be practical, thus the flowing technique to accomplish the constancy.

Both systems of nutrient solution management (OPEN or replenished CLOSED) obviously lend themselves to precise control of the nutrient solution composition so that the concentration of essential elements can be varied in response to both known physiologic states of the developing plant and the grower's sense of the condition of his crop.

There is a direct inverse relationship between flow rate and elemental concentration, i.e. the faster the flow the lower the concentration of elements needed to sustain sound plant growth. The proper relationship of these two factors within the context of a specific plant species and growing environment must be determined and maintained. This growing system is probably not, at the present time, a viable option due to the cost of pumping the nutrient solution through the rooting medium or vessel, as well as, costs for monitoring and maintaining the proper elemental ion composition of the solution. Despite these presently perceived problems, the concept is worthy of study to determine how the same "effect" can be obtained without the need to be constantly flowing and monitoring the nutrient solution. To a certain extent, NFT (see page 78) approximates the flowing concept, except NFT nutrient solution flow rates are quite slow which leads to problems in maintaining sufficient oxygen (O_2) and elemental ion concentration levels.

It is important to dwell for one moment on the problem of monitoring the composition of the solution in flowing systems. Present practice focuses principally on the solution composition of the formula selected. In point of fact, the actual ion concentration of the elements in the nutrient solution will determine whether the requirements of the plant are satisfied. The difficulty in defining what these concentrations should be was recently pointed out by two Australia plant nutritionists[9], who prepared a list giving the limiting concentrations for 9 elements in some commonly used nutrient solutions (Table 9). The wide range of concentrations found in practice can be explained by the way in which the solution is managed. This matter will be covered in more detail later.

Steiner[10] has suggested that at most only a handful of nutrient solution formulas are useful; at best, only one formula is sufficient for most plants as long as the ion balance between the elements is maintained. Steiner feels that most plants will grow extremely well in one UNIVERSAL nutrient solution with the following percentage equivalent ratios of anions and cations:

$$
\begin{array}{rl}
NO_3^- & \text{—} \quad 50 \text{ to } 70\% \text{ of the anions} \\
H_2PO_4^- & \text{—} \quad 3 \text{ to } 20\% \text{ of the anions} \\
SO_4^{--} & \text{—} \quad 25 \text{ to } 45\% \text{ of the anions} \\
K^+ & \text{—} \quad 30 \text{ to } 40\% \text{ of the cations} \\
Ca^{++} & \text{—} \quad 35 \text{ to } 55\% \text{ of the cations} \\
Mg^{++} & \text{—} \quad 15 \text{ to } 30\% \text{ of the cations}
\end{array}
$$

He also suggests that these ion concentration ratios may vary a bit as follows:

NO_3^-	:	$H_2PO_4^-$	:	SO_4^{--}
60	:	5	:	35
K^+	:	Ca^{++}	:	Mg^{++}
35	:	45	:	20

These ion ratios are graphically presented in Figure 7.

Steiner's thesis depends upon the assumption that plants can adjust to ratios of cations and anions which are not typical of their normal uptake characteristics, but that plants will expend much less energy if the ions of the essential elements are in proper balance as given above. Steiner's thesis explains, in part, why many growers have successfully grown plants using Hoagland-type nutrient solution formulas. Plants are apparently able to adjust to the composition of the nutrient solution even when the ratios of ions are not within the ranges required for best growth. Steiner also suggests that the proper balance and utilization of ions in the nutrient solution are best achieved by using his UNIVERSAL NUTRIENT SOLUTION formulas (see Table 8).

9. C.J. Asher and D.G. Edwards. 1978. Critical External Concentrations for Nutrient Deficiency and Excess. pp 13–28. IN A.R. Ferguson, R.L. Bialaski and I.B. Ferguson (Eds) Proceedings 8th International Colloquium Plant Analysis and Fertilizer Problems. Information Series No. 134, New Zealand Dept. of Scientific & Industrial Research, Wellington, New Zealand.

10. Abram A. Steiner. 1980. The Selective Capacity of Plants for Ions and its Importance for the Composition and Treatment of the Nutrient Solution. pp 37–97. IN R.G. Hurd, P. Adams, D.M. Massey and D. Price (Eds) Symposium on Research on Recirculating Water Culture. ACTA HORTICULTURE, No. 98. The Hague, The Netherlands.

TABLE 9. COMPARISON OF LIMITING CONCENTRATIONS FOR 9 ELEMENTS IN SOME NUTRIENT SOLUTIONS COMMONLY USED FOR EXPERIMENTAL PURPOSES.
(See Footnote 9 as source)

Element	Deficient	Just adequate	Toxic	Common range in nutrient solutions
.... *ppm*[1]				
Nitrogen				
as NO_3^-	0.14–10	3.0–70	20.0–200	49–210
as NH_4^+	0.007–5	0.03–25	0.4–100	0–154
Potassium				
(NH_4^+ present)	0.4–6	10–39	–	59–390
(NH_4^+ absent)	0.04–4	1.1–5		
Calcium	0.02–22	0.24–40	–	80–200
Magnesium	0.05–6	0.2–9	–	24–60
Phosphorus	0.003–4	0.007–2.6	0.03–4	15–192
Sulphur	–	1.3	–	48–224
.... *ppb*[2]				
Manganese	0.55–71	0.55–2310	16.5–3850	110–550
Zinc	0.65–3	3.25–16	195–390	0–146
Copper	0.63	1.26	–	0–10

1. ppm = parts per million.
2. ppb = parts per billion (1/1000 of ppm).

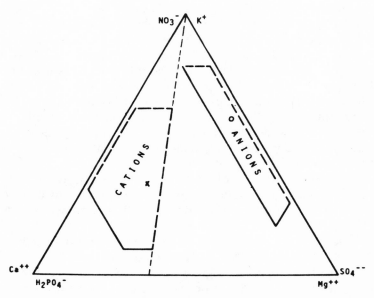

Figure 7. The composition of Steiner's universal nutrient solution (O and X) and the favourable areas for plant production.
Solid lines   = Precipitation limits at 0.7 atm. osmotic pressure and pH 6.5
broken lines = physiological limits

(Source: see footnote 10.)

One of the main theses of this book is that plants will do better if the nutrient solution is in proper ion balance with the plant's preference as suggested by Steiner. So, despite the fact that growers can raise plants with less-than-optimum solutions, proper management of the nutrient solution will produce a better plant providing better yields faster, in short, careful consideration of and attention to control of the nutrient solution will give the grower a definite financial advantage.

In a CLOSED, recirculating hydroponic system, it is necessary to add (usually daily) water to the nutrient solution in order to maintain its original volume. This is the common recommendation. However, some of the elements are removed along with the water from the nutrient solution. It is best to replace these absorbed elements by adding them to the make-up water. The question is, which elements and how much should be added?

The elements that are most likely to show the greatest change are nitrogen (N) and potassium (K), followed by several of the other major elements. A good rule of thumb is to dilute the nutrient solution formula for the major elements and add it as the make-up water, making this solution about one-third to one-half the strength of the original nutrient solution. Some experimenting and testing will be necessary to determine what that proper strength should be, so as not to create an ion imbalance by adding back too much or too little. The micronutrients should NOT be included in the make-up nutrient solution, in order to minimize the possible danger from excesses.

Some recommendations for the composition of the make-up water will be given later for particular hydroponic systems.

D. pH

The pH of the nutrient solution is thought to be best when kept between 6.0 and 6.5, although most nutrient solutions when initially constituted will have a pH between 5.0 and 6.0. It is well known that if the nutrient solution pH drops below 5.0 or goes over 7.0, plant growth may be affected. It has also been recently observed that 20 different plant species showed a similar nitrogen (N) source preference for either nitrate (NO_3^-) or ammonium (NH_4^+)-N when the pH of the nutrient solution was varied from 5.0 to 7.0. Similar experiments need to be conducted for the other essential elements to determine the effect of nutrient solution pH on elemental uptake by plants.

The pH of the nutrient solution markedly affects the availability of certain elements, particularly the micronutrients, stimulating excessive uptake at a low pH, and resulting in removal from the nutrient solution by precipitation at high pH. Therefore, careful control of the pH is important inorder both to keep all the essential elements in solution, and to prevent toxicity due to excessive uptake.

It is believed that the pH of the nutrient solution is less critical in a flowing solution culture system than in one that is static, as long as the pH remains between 5.0 and 7.0. Therefore, control of pH in flowing nutrient solution systems is substantially less demanding.

A considerable degree of pH control can be obtained by simply selecting a specific ratio of nitrate (NO_3^-) to ammonium (NH_4^+) ions when the nutrient solution is initially prepared. If the ratio of NO_3^- to NH_4^+ is greater than 9 to 1, the pH of the solution tends to increase with time, while ratios of 8 to 1 or less, pH decreases with time as illustrated in Figure 8.

Appropriate combinations of either mono- or di-hydrogen phosphate salts of either calcium (Ca) or potassium (K) will also give some degree of pH control with time.

Diurnal fluctuations in pH occur as the result of the changing solubility of carbon dioxide (CO_2) in the nutrient solution; however, these changes are usually not of sufficient magnitude to warrent daily adjustment.

The pH of the nutrient solution can be adjusted by monitoring the pH continuously or

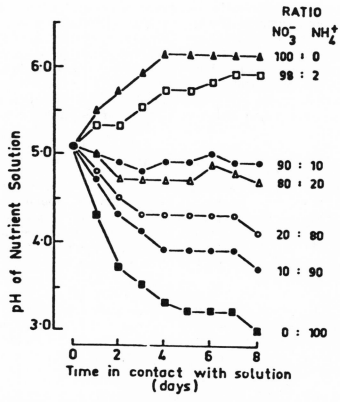

Figure 8. Effect of the ratio of nitrate to ammonium nitrogen on the rate and direction of pH changes in nutrient solutions in contact with the roots of *Triticum aestivium* plants.

(From: Trelease, S.F. and Trelease, H.M., Am. J. Bot. 22: 520–542. 1935.)

after each period of use, adding an acid or alkali, as the case requires, to lower or raise the pH. The common procedure is to continuously monitor the pH and inject acid or alkali into the flowing stream of nutrient solution. Solutions of either sodium or potassium hydroxide (NaOH, KOH) are suitable alkalis for raising the pH. Ammonium hydroxide (NH_4OH) can also be used, however, it is more difficult to handle safely and the addition of the ammonium (NH_4^+) ion to the nutrient solution may not be desired. Several acids can be used for lowering the pH. Nitric, sulphuric and hydrochloric (HNO_3, H_2SO_4, HCl) acids are quite suitable. Phosphroic acid (H_3PO_4) can also be used. Those acids and alkalis that contain one or more of the essential elements are less desirable for use than those that do not contain such elements. Thus, sodium hydroxide (NaOH) is the preferred alkali and hydrochloric acid (HCl) the preferred acid.

As was mentioned earlier (see page 33), some plants will effectively reduce the pH of the solution in the immediate vicinity of their roots. This acidification enhances their ability to absorb certain elements such as iron (Fe). If the nutrient solution is constantly being adjusted upward to neutral pH, it can interfere with the plant's natural ability to enhance its elemental ion absorptive capability. Therefore, some have suggested that the pH of the nutrient solution should not be continuously adjusted, but allowed to seek its own level naturally. This may be a desirable practice with those plant species sensitive to Fe when being grown hydroponically.

pH control of the nutrient solution may be akin to nutrient solution filtering discussed in some detail earlier (see pages 37–38). It may be that more has been made about pH control and its potential effect on plants than can be justified from actual experience. Therefore, the requirement for pH control becomes a management decision, balancing benefits gained versus costs to control. It is obvious that there are limits to which the pH of the nutrient solution should be allowed to reach, but what is needed to maintain the pH from reaching those extremes may be academic since within normal experience with most nutrient solution formulas and their requirements for use, these extremes are seldom reached.

E. USE

The hydroponic or soilless grower's objective is to supply the growing crop by means of the nutrient solution, its elemental and water requirements without inducing stress, and to do so at a reasonable cost. The composition and schedule of use for the nutrient solution must be responsive to both crop demand and also the constraints inherent in the technique of delivery. Those CLOSED systems which recirculate the nutrient solution require careful management to avoid large shifts in pH and elemental composition between scheduled supplementation or renewal.

In the presence of a rooting media, accumulation of elements in the media by absorption or precipitation must be minimized by frequent leaching of the media with pure water, as well as by adjustments in the formula and use of the nutrient solution. Obviously, accumulation must be dealt with to avoid elemental imbalances, and consequent deficiencies or toxicities. These and other aspects of nutrient solution management are discussed in this section.

Temperature: The temperature of the nutrient solution should never be less than the ambient air temperature, particularly in systems where plant roots are exposed to intermittent surges of a large volume of nutrient solution. On warm days when the atmospheric demand on the plants is high, root contact with nutrient solution below ambient temperature results in plant wilting. Plant roots, sitting in cool or cold nutrient solution, can not absorb sufficient water and elements to meet the demand imposed by warm air and bright sunshine. Repeated exposure to cool nutrient solution results in below expected plant growth and performance, evidenced by poor fruit set and quality, and delayed maturity. In such circumstances, it is necessary to warm the nutrient solution to avoid cold stress. On the other hand, when air temperature is low, a warm nutrient solution will not only do no harm but will help maintain plant growth, as does soil heating in conventional growing systems. A good rule of thumb is to maintain the solution in the 68°C–86°F range. A more detailed discussion on the effect of rooting temperature on water and elemental uptake may be found on page 34.

pH: The necessity to establish and maintain a desirable pH for the nutrient solution has already been discussed (see pages 48–50). The pH of newly constituted solution is usually in the proper range since this is one of the objectives of most nutrient solution formulas. Recirculation of used solution can, however, lead to major shifts in pH which, if allowed to go beyond the recommended range, can lead to possible detrimental effects on plant growth and yield. However, with normal use of the nutrient solution, these extremes may not be reached, making daily pH adjustment unnecessary. However, daily monitoring of the nutrient solution is recommended and adjustment made when extremes have been reached.

Soluble Salts: Most nutrient solution formulas have a fairly low osmotic pressure when initially made. The SALT EFFECT can be minimized by selecting those compounds that have low salt indices (see Table 10) when making the nutrient solution. It is with use and/or reuse that the SOLUBLE SALT problem arises. This problem develops when substantial quantities of water are removed from the nutrient solution at a very rapid rate as happens on hot, low humidity days. If not replaced, the osmotic pressure of the nutrient solution rises very rapidly. This problem can become particularly acute if the nutrient solution is being recirculated and the water lost due to evapotranspiration is not quickly replaced.

The problem of soluble salts also develops in soilless systems using rooting media. Elements tend to accumulate differentially in most rooting media subjected to repeated application of nutrient solution. This problem is corrected by flushing the rooting media with pure water to remove the accumulated salts. Flushing frequency varies with the system of growing employed and the growing media used. Salt accumulations are usually monitored by measuring the conductivity of effluent from the rooting medium (see Table 11). When the conductivity reaches a predetermined level, the medium is leached with pure water. Frequent monitoring and effective leaching are important practices for all soilless growing systems.

TABLE 10. RELATIVE SALT INDEX FOR COMMON CHEMICAL FORMS USED FOR PREPARING NUTRIENT SOLUTIONS

Compound	Formula	Relative salt index*
Ammonium nitrate	NH_4NO_3	104
Ammonium sulfate	$(NH_4)_2SO_4$	69
Calcium nitrate	$Ca(NO_3)_2$	52
Calcium sulfate	$CaSO_4$	8
Diammonium phosphate	$(NH_4)_2HPO_4$	29
Monoammonium phosphate	$NH_4H_2PO_4$	34
Monocalcium phosphate	$CaHPO_4$	15
Potassium chloride	KCl	116
Potassium nitrate	KNO_3	73
Potassium sulfate	K_2SO_4	46
Sodium nitrate	$NaNO_3$	100

*The index is relative to an equivalent amount of sodium nitrate.

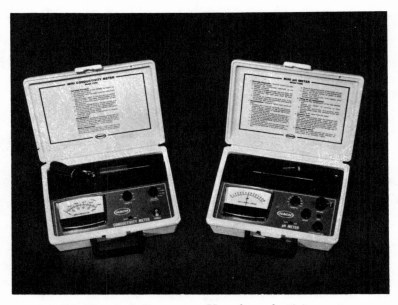

HACH Chemical Company pH and conductivity meters.

TABLE 11. ELECTRICAL CONDUCTIVITY MEASUREMENT AND INTERPRETATION

Definition:

Conductivity is a measure of the electrical resistance of water, nutrient solution, or effluent from a growing bed or container, used to determine the content of ions in solution to describe levels from deficiency to excess. Electrical conductivity is determined using a standard CONDUCTANCE CELL and salt bridge, the reading being expressed as:

$$\text{SPECIFIC CONDUCTANCE (L, mmhos/cm)} = \frac{\text{cell constant } (\theta)}{\text{resistance (ohms)}}$$

The common methods of expression for L are:

millimhos (mmhos) —mhos $\times 10^{-3}$/cm
*   —mhos $\times 10^{-5}$/cm
micromhos (umhos)—mhos $\times 10^{-6}$/cm

*this method of expression is used to give whole numbers rather than decimals when expressed as mmhos.
(Example: 0.1 mmhos = 10 mhos $\times 10^{-5}$)

Conversions:

Osmotic Pressure (atms) = $0.28 - 0.36 \, L_{mmhos/cm}$
Milliequivalents of salt/liter = $12.5 \, L_{mmhos/cm}$
Parts per million of salts = $640 \, L_{mmhos/cm}$

Interpretation:

(a) Expected Effects of Salt Crop Growth.

Conductivity of saturation extract (mmho/cm)	Total salt content (%)	Crop reaction	Classification
<2	<0.1	Salinity effects mostly negligible	Nonsaline
2–4	0.1–0.15	Yields of very sensitive crops may be restricted	Slightly saline
4–8	0.15–0.35	Yields of many crops restricted	Moderately saline
8–16	0.35–0.70	Only tolerant crops yield satisfactorily	Very saline
>16	>0.70	Only a few very tolerant crops yield satisfactorily	Extremely saline

(Source: Diagnosis and Improvement of Saline and Alkaline Soils. Agricultural Handbook No. 60. USDA, U.S. Government Printing Office, Washington, D.C., 1954.)

(b) Specific Conductance of Saturated Extract from Organic Growth Media

Specific conductance mmhos/cm	Interpretation
0–0.75	Low
0.75–2.00	Acceptable
2.00–3.50	Optimum
3.50–5.00	High
5.00 +	Very High

(Source: Handbook on Reference Methods for Soil Testing, 1980. Council on Soil Testing and Plant Analysis, Athens, Georgia.)

(c) Nutrition Solution: Most nutrient solutions have specific conductances ranging from 3.0 to 7.0 mmhos/cm which make them moderately saline in terms of possible crop response. The SPECIFIC CONDUCTANCE may be determined initially, and with nutrient solution use, SPECIFIC CONDUCTANCE used to replenish the nutrient solution with suspected spent elements.

(d) Water: Source water used to prepare the nutrient solution should not have a SPECIFIC CONDUCTANCE greater than 6.0 mmhos/cm. If so, then there is the possibility of plant damage due to excessive SALTS, particularly for those crops that are sensitive to salt.

(e) Tolerance of Three Types of Crops for Salinity. Under each of the three types of crops the most tolerant crops are listed first and the least tolerant last.

		Salt Tolerance		
Type of crop	Tolerant (Group I)	Moderately tolerant to moderately sensitive (Group II)		Sensitive (Group III)
Fruit	Date palm	Pomegranate Fig Grape Olive		Lemon Grapefruit Pear Almond Apricot Peach Plum Apple Orange
Field and truck	Sugar beet Garden beet Milo Rape Kale Lettuce Alfalfa	Alfalfa Flax Tomato Asparagus Foxtail millet Sorghum (grain) Barley (grain) Rye (grain) Oats (grain) Rice	Cantaloupe Sweet potato Sunflower Carrot Spinach Squash Sugar cane Corn Onion Pepper	Vetch Peas Celery Cabbage Artichoke Eggplant Sweet potato Potato Green beans Black walnut

			Wheat (grain) Cotton Potato	Pecan
Forage	Alkali sacaton Salt grasses Nuttall alkali Bermuda Rhodes Rescue Canada wild rye Beardless wild rye Western wheat grass Barley (hay)	White sweet clover Yellow sweet clover Perennial rye grass Mountain brome Barley (hay) Birdsfoot trefoil Strawberry clover Dallis grass Sudan grass Hubam clover Alfalfa (California common) Tall fescue Rye (hay)	Wheat (hay) Oats (hay) Orchard grass Blue grama Meadow fescue Reed canary Big trefoil Smooth brome Tall meadow oat grass Cicer milk vetch Sour clover Sickle milk vetch	White Dutch clover Meadow foxtail Alsike clover Red clover Ladino clover Burnet

(Source: Irrigation Principles and Practices, 4th Edition. 1979. V.E. Hanson, O.W. Israelsen and G.E. Stringham. John Wiley & Sons, New York, NY.)

Application Techniques: How a nutrient solution is used profoundly impacts its composition. There are essentially four distinct application techniques:

DRIP
INTERMITTENT FLOW
CONTINUOUS FLOW
AERATED STANDING

Each of these technique impose certain constraints on the way in which the nutrient solution is initially made and subsequently renewed. The complexity of nutrient solution management becomes clear when the effects of application technique are considered in the context of container volume ratios and the effects of the growing plants. All of these factors significantly modify the nutrient solution composition.

Our knowledge of all these complex reactions is insufficient to predetermine all the possible outcomes in terms of plant growth and vigor. Only relative or approximate recommendations can be given to guide the grower in modifying the composition and use of the nutrient solution to meet the specific crop requirement-system needs. Beyond the recommendations which follow, the grower should look to diagnostic procedures, and a plant and nutrient solution analyses (see pages 88–92 and 95, respectively), for guidance in modifying the nutrient solution in terms of his specific system.

DRIP

Drip application is widely used with several types of media systems. The nutrient solution is applied to the rooting medium at a rate sufficient to meet the water requirement of the plant, but without saturating the medium. Either a complete nutrient solution, such as Hoagland's (see Table 6), or one containing only those elements not found in the rooting medium is used. Drip culture for organic soilless mix systems is discussed on pages 71–72. The same general technique is equally applicable to inorganic media systems, following essentially the same techniques for making and managing the nutrient solution.

Soluble salt build-up tends to develop quickly in drip systems. Therefore, the effluent should be closely monitored and the rooting medium leached frequently to prevent high salt accumulation.

It is worth mentioning that drip irrigation (sometimes referred to as trickle irrigation), is becoming a world-wide technique for irrigating large fields. It is today the major technique for irrigating crops grown in the many desert areas of the world[11]. Drip irrigation is the only practical method for precisely applying water and essential elements when irrigation is required to grow a crop. But, the technique is not without its problems and high cost. Drip systems require precision pumps, an intricate distribution system and controlled release devices. Clogging, leaks and ineffective control are constant problems for the user. However, drip systems are gaining in use, becoming a major method for water and essential element application for crops grown in the field and in soilless culture. In soilless culture, drip irrigation systems are replacing the formerly used overhead irrigation procedures, particularly in the growing of ornamental plants in containers.

INTERMITTENT FLOW

Intermittent flow refers to those systems where the growing bed is periodically flooded with nutrient solution. In this system, make-up water must be added daily to maintain the original volume of solution. The common practice is to use the nutrient solution for a short period, normally 5 to 10 days, then discard it, and replace with freshly made solution. During the short life of a particular batch, the solution volume is daily restored by pure water additions, and the pH of the solution adjusted if needed, but with no attempt to restore its original elemental ion composition. The Hoagland type nutrient solution formulas work quite well with the intermittent flow system as long as the plant/volume ratio and replenishment schedules do not markedly depart from the regime described by Hoagland and Arnon[6].

The same danger from salt build-up occurs in any bed system bathed with nutrient solution, and the same precautions and leaching requirements are necessary as that described earlier (see page 51).

Intermittent flow has application to the hydroponic techniques, Nutrient Flow (NFT) and aeroponics where the nutrient solution is brought into contact with plant roots on a periodic schedule. Both of these systems for plant growing are discussed in greater detail in Chapter IX.

CONTINUOUS FLOW

Continuous flow systems are more difficult to describe in terms of nutrient solution composition since the rate of flow is a significant governing factor. As the rate of flow increases, the concentration of the elements in the nutrient solution must be reduced to avoid toxicities. It is possible in these systems to maintain the nutrient solution close to its

11. Eshel Bresler. 1977. Trickle-Drip Irrigation: Principles and Application to Soil-Water Management. pp 343–393. *IN* N.C. Brady (Ed). ADVANCES IN AGRONOMY. Academic Press, Inc., New York, New York.

initial concentration by injecting specific elements into the solution at approximately the same rate as they are removed by plant root absorption. The approximate rate of injection can be determined either by continuous analysis of the solution or estimating usage based upon past tracking records.

The rapid continuous flow of a nutrient solution has in recent years gained in popularity and use for studies in plant nutrition research. However, little has been done to apply the system to commercial growing, due mainly to the high cost of circulating the nutrient solution at the rapid rates required, rates which range as high as 480 gallons (2160 liters)/vessel/day. Considerable reduction of the elemental concentrations in the nutrient solution are required to prevent toxicities. Asher and Edwards[12] have summarized the guidelines used by a number of researchers familiar with continuous flow systems to obtain acceptable concentrations (Table 9). Note that the elemental concentrations are in some cases less than 1/10th those used in typical Hoagland-type nutrient solutions.

The most significant recent development employing continuous flow is the introduction by Cooper of the system which is called NUTRIENT FILM TECHNIQUE (NFT)[7]. It was

TABLE 12. THEORETICALLY IDEAL CONCENTRATION (ppm) OF ELEMENTS IN NUTRIENT SOLUTION FOR NFT CROPPING.

Element	Concentration, ppm
Nitrogen	200
Phosphorus	60
Potassium	300
Calcium	170
Magnesium	50
Iron	12
Manganese	2
Boron	0.3
Copper	0.1
Molybdenum	0.2
Zinc	0.1

Weights of chemical reagents to be dissovled in 1000 liters of water to give theoretically ideal concentrations

Chemical reagent	Formula	Weight, grams
Potassium dihydrogen phosphate	KH_2PO_4	263
Potassium nitrate	KNO_3	583
Calcium nitrate	$Ca(NO_3)_2 \cdot 4H_2O$	1003
Magnesium sulphate	$MgSO_4 \cdot 7H_2O$	513
EDTA iron	$[CH_2 \cdot N(CH_2 \cdot COO)_2]_2FeNa$	79
Manganous sulphate	$MnSO_4 \cdot H_2O$	6.1
Boric acid	H_3BO_3	1.7
Copper sulphate	$CuSO_4 \cdot 5H_2O$	0.39
Ammonium molybdate	$(NH_4)_6Mo_7O_{24} \cdot 4H_2O$	0.37
Zinc sulphate	$ZnSO_4 \cdot 7H_2O$	0.44

12. Colin J. Asher and David G. Edwards. 1978. Relevance of Dilute Solution Culture Studies to Problems of Low Fertility Tropical Soils. pp 131–152. IN C.S. Andrew and E.J. Kamprath (Eds) Mineral Nutrition of Legumes in Tropical and Subtropical Soils. Commonwealth Scientific & Industrial Research Organization, Melbourne, Australia.

mentioned earlier and will be discussed in more detail later (see pages 78–82). The nutrient solution flow rate is slow to minimize the cost of pumping. The speed of flow is dependent on the rate of introduction into the rooting trough, trough slope (the nutrient solution moves by gravity down the channel) and the size of the root mat in the trough. Cooper has specified a nutrient solution formula which he believes is best suited to the NFT system (see Table 12). It should be noted that Cooper's formula is not markedly different from those recommended for other CLOSED hydroponic systems which recirculate the nutrient solution.

A recent innovation of the NFT technique suggests that an intermittent flow of nutrient solution is more desirable than constant flow. These comparisons will be made in greater detail later in Chapter IX.

AERATED STANDING

The aerated standing nutrient solution technique is the standard procedure used for years by researchers to study the effects of elements in a nutrient solution on plants, and for growing plants when a controlled uniform rooting environment is desired. The procedure is to suspend the plant roots in an aerated nutrient solution. Water is added daily to maintain the initial volume. The nutrient solution is replenished on e, then a 5-, 7-, 10-day schedule. The solution is continuously aerated not only to maintain an adequate oxygen (O_2) supply at the roots but also to stir the solution.

The volume of nutrient solution per plant varies considerably from less than ¼ gallon (1 liter) to several gallons, depending upon the system and research objectives. The composition of the nutrient solution is usually not much different from that of Hoagland's (see Table 6). The nutrient solution can be easily monitored for elemental content. The entire solution is replaced when one or more of the elements is reduced below acceptable levels. This system of growing hydroponically is not well suited for commercial application since water and chemical use are quite high due to frequent replacement. In addition, the constantly changing composition of the nutrient solution imposes a substantial burden on the grower to maintain proper and adequate elemental ion balance and sufficiency.

Make-Up Water. In CLOSED hydroponic systems in which the nutrient solution is recirculated and make-up water is added to replace that lost by transpiration, the use of a dilute form of the initial nutrient solution as the make-up water is becoming the general practice. It is being done because a portion of the elements in the nutrient solution have been adsorbed and must be replaced to maintain the proper concentration and ion balance of the essential elements. The exact composition of make-up nutrient solutions depends on past experience and/or frequent analysis of the nutrient solution in use. The composition of a recommended "topping-up solution" is given in Table 13.

The increasingly common practice of using a dilution of the original nutrient solution formula, normally without the micronutrient portion, as the procedure for maintaining the initial volume of solution, is becoming the standard rule rather than the exception. However, there is some danger from this practice if some degree of control is not exercised, either by monitoring the elemental concentration and replacing only those elements significantly reduced in concentration, or by using a special concentration suite of elements based on anticipated need; for example, adding back only nitrogen (N) and potassium (K), the two elements frequently reduced in concentration in significant amounts.

However, no matter what system is used, great care is needed to ensure that imbalances are not created by make-up elemental additions, leaving the nutrient solution in worse condition than if only water had been used to restore the initial volume.

TABLE 13. COMPOSITION OF NUTRIENT SOLUTION FOR THE GROWING OF TOMATO AND CUCUMBER IN A NFT SYSTEM

Composition of Starting Solution

Salt	Formula	Stock solution (g.p.l.)	Dilution (ml.p.l.)	Concentration (p.p.m.)
Calcium nitrate	$Ca(NO_3)_2\ 4H_2O$	787	1.25	117 (N) 168 (Ca)
Potassium nitrate	KNO_3	169	3.9	254 (K) 91 (N)
Magnesium sulphate	$MgSO_4\ 7H_2O$	329	1.5	49 (Mg)
Potassium phosphate	KH_2PO_4	91	3.0	62 (P) 78 (K)
Chelated iron	FeNa EDTA	12.3	3.0	5.6 (Fe)
Manganese sulphate	$MnSO_{49}\ 4H_2O$	3.0	3.0	2.2 (Mn)
Boric acid	H_3BO_3	1.23	1.5	0.32 (B)
Copper sulphate	$CuSO_4\ 5H_2O$	0.17	1.5	0.065 (Cu)
Ammonium molybdate	$(NH_4)_6Mo_7O_{24}\ 4H_2O$	0.06	1.5	0.007 (Mo)
Phosphoric acid	H_3PO_3	—	0.044	23 (P)

Composition of Topping-up Solution

Salt	Formula	Stock Solution (g.p.l.)	Dilution (ml.p.l.)	Concentration (p.p.m.)
Calcium nitrate	$Ca(NO_3)_2\ 4H_2O$	787	0.5 tomatoes	47 (N) 67 (Ca)
			1.0 cucumbers	93 (N) 133 (Ca)
Magnesium sulphate	$MgSO_4\ 7H_2O$	329	1.0	32 (Mg)
Potassium nitrate	KNO_3	169	2.13	147 (K) 51 (N)
Chelated iron	FeNa EDTA	24.5	0.4 tomatoes	1.5 (Fe)
			0.8 cucumbers	3.0 (Fe)
Manganese sulphate	$MnSO_4\ 4H_2O$	7.42	0.3 tomatoes	0.55 (Mn)
			0.6 cucumbers	1.1 (Mn)
Copper sulphate	$CuSO_4\ 5H_2O$	1.7	0.15	0.065 (Cu)
Ammonium molybdate	$(NH_4)_6Mo_7O_{24}\ 4H_2O$	0.6	0.15	0.007 (Mo)
Boric acid	H_3BO_3	6.17	0.3	0.32 (B)

Source: Commercial Applications of NFT. 1979. Growers Books, 49 Doughty Street, London, England WC1N 2LP.

F. CROP SPECIES REQUIREMENTS

Little has been said up to this point about the requirements for adjusting the composition of the nutrient solution for various crop species. For some growers this is not an important requirement which means that the commonly published nutrient solution formulas (see Table 7) are suitable for most crops. Experience would seem to justify such a conclusion. However, this is not entirely true, particularly for the element nitrogen (N). Fruiting crops, such as tomato and cucumber which are commonly grown hydroponically, have different N requirements which also vary with the stage of growth. It is common practice to begin with a lower concentration of N in the nutrient solution, less than 100 ppm; and when fruit set begins, increase this concentration to 150 ppm; and then to 175 ppm during the latter stages of fruit production. For cucumber, the third increase in N concentration in the nutrient solution is not recommended. Even though the N concentration in the nutrient solution is increased, that of the other elements is not: their concentration is held at that initially specified. It is also common practice to begin a crop of tomato or cucumber on half-strength nutrient solution until the first flowers appear, and then increase to full strength for the remaining period of growth and fruit production.

If the N concentration in the nutrient solution is increased as suggested above, it is necessary to carefully monitor the nutrient solution to ensure that the other major elements in the solution are not depleted during its use. Particular attention should be given to K, maintaining its initial concentration by supplemental additions if necessary, since this element is closely related to fruit quality.

Another crop commonly grown hydroponically is lettuce. This crop can tolerate and requires fairly high N concentrations in the nutrient solution, and less attention is required to maintain a proper balance between N and the other major elements, such as K when growing tomato and cucumber.

Relatively little is known about the nutrient solution requirements related to the production of flowers and other ornamental plants. For example, chrysanthemum, commonly hydroponically grown, does well on a number of nutrient solution formulas. Similarly, despite known differences in elemental requirements, other plant species grow well in the common nutrient solutions. The important requirement is to maintain the initial balance and concentration of the essential elements given in the formula during the use of any particular batch. Therefore, for most of these non-food crops, nutrient solution composition maintenance seems to be the critical factor rather than the elemental concentration called for in the formula. What is being realized is a fulfilment of Steiner's[8] assertion that plants have the ability "to select the ions in the mutual ratio favourable for their growth and development" from most nutrient solutions.

It is easy to assume that since most plants do quite well on nutrient solution formulas in common use today that further investigation and development will yield little value. I submit that this is not so. I suggest that little correlation between plant specie growth response and nutrient solution composition has been observed to date only because of other interfering and limiting factors. It is only when all the factors affecting plant growth are at their optimum that presently unobserved influences suddenly appear. In the past, most growers were quite satisfied with average responses from their systems of growing. But, when they begin to reach for maximum potential, they will discover that precision in each procedure employed makes a difference. When growers reach this point in their crop production systems, hydroponic or otherwise, the care in making and managing the nutrient solution may become the crucial factor in determining their success. In short, most growers have yet to approach levels of maximum growth potential where the plant specie/nutrient solution composition makes a difference.

Chapter VIII: Systems of Soilless Media Culture

There are a number of ways to grow plants by means of soilless culture. For purposes of this book, I follow the classification scheme offered by Dr. John Larsen of the Texas Agricultural Extension Service (Figure 9). In his classification system, hydroponics is one distinct technique for plant growing where no root supporting medium is used.

As already indicated, growing plants hydroponically is different for systems which employ a support or rooting medium as compared to non-medium systems. Management of the nutrient solution for these two classes of systems is quite different. It is important, however, to keep in mind not only the differences, but also, the similarities between these practices, as some of the management procedures can be successfully transferred, while others cannot. This chapter begins with media culture techniques, those which have and/or are in commercial use, and concludes with techniques that have yet to be brought into commercial use, but which offer great promise for successful hydroponic growing in the future.

SOILLESS CULTURE

Hydroponics or Water Culture	Media Culture		
	Organic	Inorganic	Mixtures
1. NFT (Nutrient Film Technique)	1. Peat moss	1. Gravel	1. Peat-vermiculite
2. Aeroponics (misting roots)	2. Pine bark	2. Hadite	2. Pine bark-vermiculite
	3. Rice hulls	3. Lava Rock	3. etc.
3. Continually aerated nutrient solution	4. etc.	4. Vermiculite	
		5. etc.	

Figure 9. Dr. John Larsen's Soilless Culture Classification System.

A. CONTAINER GROWING

All forms of soilless culture involve growing plants in some kind of a container—a bed, pot, bag, can or trough. The size or dimensions of the rooting vessel is frequently chosen on the basis of convenience or availability. The Number 10 food can is an example of convenience and availability which has resulted in its selection and wide use. More recently, the so-called "gallon" and "2-gallon" (actual volumes are 3 and 6 quarts, respectively) containers have become popular. Today, it is not unusual to find growers placing a soilless medium in a free-standing plastic bag and using this as the growing container, or growing directly in the bag that is used to package an organic soilless mix as shown in Figure 10.

In many hydroponic gravel bed and trough systems, insufficient volume for root extension results in unusual root development. For example, roots wind their way into pipes and drains which bring the nutrient solution to and from the bed, restricting solution flow and making clean-up between crops difficult. In most trough systems, such as NFT, the container volume available for root development becomes insufficient as the rooting mat begins to fill the trough, restricting nutrient solution flow and reducing aeration which leads to poor plant performance.

Therefore, the primary objective in determining the size and dimensions for the rooting vessel, trough or bed, should be to provide adequate space for normal root growth and development.

Figure 10. "Bag Culture" technique by growing plants in shipping bag of organic soilless mix.

Plant root appearance and growth habit are different in different rooting environments. Tomato plant roots, for example, will be fibrous, long and numerous when growing in a peat-lite organic soilless mix; course, short and few in number in pure pine bark; and long, course and relatively few in number in a hydroponic gravel culture system. This suggests that a tomato plant will grow quite well in a relatively small container containing a soilless organic mix like pine bark, but will require a larger container for a peat-lite mix. I have obtained good growth and production of tomato and cucumber grown in the greenhouse, and a variety of garden vegetables in outdoor grow-boxes, when grown in a 7-inch depth of pure pine bark. I have also found that when tomato plants are grown in pots with plastic mesh liners between the medium and pot wall (to prevent the roots from extending beyond the plastic mesh), top growth was directly proportional to pot size. The restricted root growth produced a "bonsai" effect.

It is surprising how little good information is available on the importance of rooting volume required by plants and the relationship that exists between the rooting habit, and container environment and volume. It has been thought that root appearance is associated with plant performance, i.e., the larger root mat in terms of number of roots, their length and the number of fibrous roots, the better the performance of the plant. Such a view is not entirely true. A healthy root system may assume a variety of physical characteristics. But one characteristic is essential as an indicator of root health, namely color. Clear white roots indicates "active live" roots. Dark colored roots indicates "inactive or dead" roots.

Despite uncertainties about the relation of physical appearance to root performance, there are some guidelines that will assist the grower in determining the rooting volume needed for the crop and system being employed.

1. For all containers, the depth should be one and a half to two times the diameter of the surface area covered by the plant canopy when the plant reaches its maximum size. For example, if the canopy covers (or will cover) a surface area 12 inches in diameter, then the growing container should be 18 to 24 inches deep.
2. In bed culture systems, increased spacing between plants can, in part, substitute for a lesser depth. For example, plants with a canopy occupying a surface area 12 inches in diameter growing in a bed less than 12 inches deep should be spaced 18 inches from one plant center to another. This ratio of 2 to 3 can be applied to plants with smaller or larger canopies when growing in bed systems.

It is generally accepted that roots of neighboring plants inhibit each other's growth. Therefore, close contact and intermingling of roots between neighboring plants, the result of too close spacing or shallow rooting depth, should be minimized by providing the area and depth required.

Some feel that the present lack of knowledge of root growth in varying environments restricts our knowledge of plant growth in general. I would agree! The consequences for the soilless culture grower is that he must experiment with his growing system to determine the rooting volume required to obtain maximum plant performance. Beginning with the recommendations given above, plants can be spaced closer together until there appears a significant change in plant growth and yield.

Needless to say, root volume requirement becomes academic when plants must be widely spaced to allow sufficient light to penetrate the plant canopy for those plants that are widely branched and/or grow tall.

B. INORGANIC MEDIA SOILLESS CULTURE

The use of gravel or sand beds in a CLOSED recirculating nutrient solution system is probably the oldest of all the commercial soilless culture systems as shown in Figure 11. It was widely used from the 1930s to the 1950s and remains in use on a limited basis today. A significant modification of the basic system is the sand bed built on a slanting platform through which the nutrient solution flows from the upper to the lower end in an OPEN one-way passage by gravity as shown in Figure 12. The main advantage of both techniques is that they can be expanded readily. There seem to be no limits to size. However, the disadvantages are significant. These systems are very inefficient in the use of both water and the essential elements. The common CLOSED management procedure is to use the nutrient solution 1–2 weeks, and then dump and remake. Then, the entire system must be flushed with pure water before introducing the new batch of nutrient solution. This flushing is both time consuming and requires sizeable quantities of water. The slanted sand bed system is quite efficient in its use of nutrient solution and water during the growing cycle but not during flushing.

Another technique used with sand beds is to introduce the nutrient solution through a drip system which better controls water and elemental use, and also means less flushing out of unspent accumulating elements. Water and elements are applied only in the vicinity of the rooting mass. Flushing of the sand bed must be done, although less frequently.

Even with routine flushing, unused salts accumulate on the media which will eventually and significantly affect the composition of the nutrient solution. The elements,

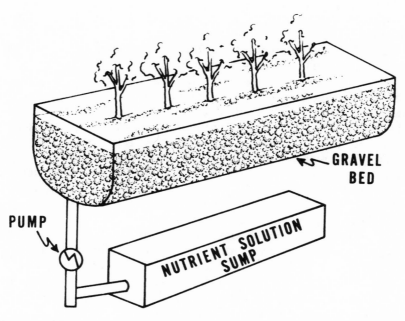

Figure 11. Gravel bed-sump nutrient solution system for soilless growing

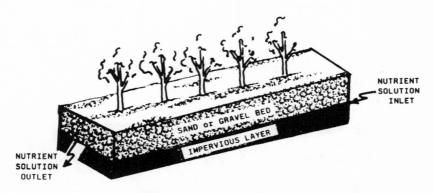

Figure 12. Slanting sand or gravel bed soilless culture system.

calcium (Ca), phosphorus (P), and the micronutrients, copper (Cu), iron (Fe), manganese (Mn) and zinc (Zn), precipitate on the surface of gravel or sand particles. This accumulation can be easily observed as a white or grayish mud-like substance that adheres to your hand when you run it through the bed. It is possible to compensate for this accumulation by making each successive nutrient solution batch in such a way that an increasing degree of reliance is placed on the accumulated elements in the beds as a source for the needed elements. However, this approach requires considerable skill and care in monitoring the amount of salt accumulation and in properly adjusting subsequent nutrient solution batches. Frequently, in spite of these major adjustments, unsatisfactory plant growth results. The problem of accumulation in the rooting media will become sufficiently acute in time that the medium must be discarded and replaced with fresh gravel or sand.

Another major problem, but one not unique to gravel and sand bed culture alone, is disease control. If a disease organism is introduced into the nutrient solution, it will be carried throughout the entire system. It is not uncommon to see an entire crop wiped out due to the rapid spread of disease. It is practically impossible to control a disease once established in the system, therefore great care must be exercised to prevent its introduction. Equally difficult is the enormous task of cleaning-up after a disease infestation. Normally, the entire system must be sterilized.

Furthermore, it must be pointed out that the nutrient solution is expected to provide both the water and essential elements needed by the plant. It is easily and erroneously assumed that these two physiologic requirements occur in tandem. In fact on warm days when plants are transpiring rapidly, only water is needed to meet the atmospheric demand; but nutritional elements are not required by the crop in other than usual amounts. Commonly the FEEDING CYCLE, meaning the flow of the nutrient solution through the growing bed, is used to meet the plant's need for water. The consequence is that the need for water is out of phase with the feeding cycle. This juxtaposition of events poises a major problem for the grower since it is not common to have a water-only system operating in parallel with the nutrient solution delivery system. Therefore, the only thing the grower can do is recirculate the nutrient solution which leads to over-feeding the plants, and a possible risk of elemental imbalance and accumulation.

In such a situation, water only should be added to the sump to maintain the initial volume of the solution since a diluted form of the nutrient solution for make-up enhances the accumulation of elements in and on the medium. This recommendation, oriented to a specific set of conditions, must not be confused with the recommendation oriented to typical conditions which calls for the addition of a dilute form of the nutrient solution as make-up water in a CLOSED system (see page 57).

Substitutes for gravel or sand as root support media have been tried, but most are quite expensive or not suited for large installations, so have little to commend them. Perlite and volcanic rock are two such recently introduced materials. They have been suggested primarily for use in small growing units, such as systems which use PVC piping in a rack arrangement with the upper larger pipe serving as the growing bed and the smaller lower pipe as the nutrient solution sump as shown in Figure 13. The nutrient solution is pumped periodically from the sump into the growing bed pipe and then allowed to return by gravity flow. Being a CLOSED system, the nutrient solution must be replaced periodically, usually about every 5th to 7th day.

Figure 13. Growing plants in a bed-sump system made of PVC piping with a fish pump circulation system.
(Supplied by U.S. Agro Systems, 409 Union Ave., Holbrook, New York 11741.)

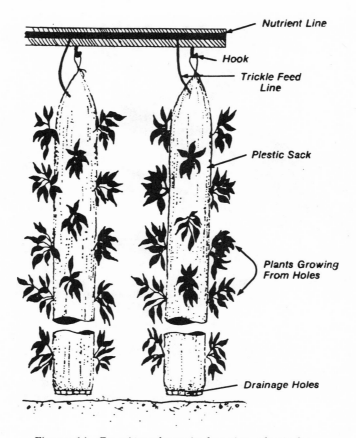

Figure 14. Growing plants in hanging plastic bags containing perlite or similar material being supplied with nutrient solution.

(Source: H.M. Resh. Hydroponic Food Production. Second Edition by Howand M. Desh 198 Woodbridge Press. Santa Barbara, California.)

A recently introduced system using inorganic media involves passing of nutrient solution through vertical tubes containing perlite with plants, such as lettuce or strawberries, growing from openings on the sides of the tubes as shown in Figure 14. Another involves growing plants in blocks of rockwool with the nutrient solution dripped onto the block or flowing the nutrient solution past the blocks placed in troughs as shown in Figure 15. Both systems seem to work quite well. Being OPEN systems, the nutrient solution is used in a one-way passage in order to avoid both the hazards and costs of recirculation.

The most common nutrient solution formula used in inorganic soilless systems is Hoagland's (see Table 6), or something close to it. The typical concentration range for the major elements is:

Element	Concentration, ppm
N	100–150
P	30–40
K	130–180
Ca	90–150
Mg	30–50

The micronutrient formula is universally Hoagland's (see Table 6).

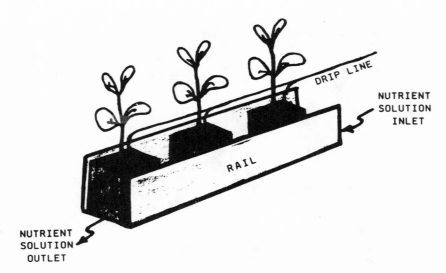

Figure 15. Growing plants in blocks (or cubes) of rock wool or other similar material in a rail with flowing nutrient solution, or alternately the nutrient solution may be dripped on each individual block.

These concentration ranges for the major elements work well for most crops and growing systems. In large CLOSED systems, the procedure recommended is to monitor the nutrient solution daily, adjust the pH if outside the desired range and maintain the initial volume by adding dilute nutrient solution. pH adjustment is called for only to keep the solution pH between 5.5. and 6.5. The make-up water should be either ¼ or ½ strength nutrient solution less the micronutrients, or some other solution based on a determination of the elements required or some other special solution (see pages 39, 48). The nutrient solution is entirely discarded after 10 to 14 days use.

In smaller CLOSED systems, the nutrient solution pH is not to be adjusted, pure water is added to maintain the initial volume and the entire solution is discarded after 5 to 7 days use.

In all CLOSED systems, it is advisable to flush the growing bed with pure water between each nutrient solution change. After the nutrient solution is dumped, the sump is filled with pure water and circulated as nutrient solution for one day. Then this water is discard and the sump filled with fresh nutrient solution.

In OPEN systems, the growing bed, bag or blocks should be periodically leached with pure water to remove accumulated salts. The determination, as to when leaching is needed, is based on a determination of the conductivity (see Table 11) of the eluted nutrient solution. If the conductivity is greater than that of the fresh nutrient solution, leaching is needed.

C. ORGANIC MEDIA SOILLESS CULTURE

The use of organic substances, such as sphagnum peatmoss, pine bark, straw, etc., is becoming extremely popular for soilless plant growing. These organic rooting media have the advantages of low cost and ease of use. It is common practice to add a mixture of other materials including vermiculite, perlite and sand to the organic substrate to provide desired characteristics, such as, increased porosity, water holding capacity or weight. Although much has been said and written about the constitution of a DESIRABLE mix, little data to substantiate these claims has been produced. Most growers depend upon past experience or that of others when selecting or making their own mix.

Organic media have physical and chemical properties that make their use unique as compared to inorganic media. For example, sphagnum peatmoss and pine bark exhibit to some degree both adsorptive and absorptive properties. So they act more like soil, characteristics not found in the inorganic substances, such as gravel or sand. These organic substances provide a buffering capacity which can work to the advantage of the grower, serving as a storage mechanism for the essential elements which both reduces the likelihood of elemental excesses and shortages. In addition, the organic substances used may intrinsically contain some of the essential elements required by plants in sufficient quantity to satisfy the crop requirement. All of these factors must be taken into account when planning which essential elements are to be added to the mix, and in what quantities and form, to optimize plant growth and crop yield.

The grower is well advised to have typical samples tested to identify those elements contained in the media and their concentration before using an organic substrate. Such tests will provide a useful basis for planning which system of nutrient solution management is best (see pages 92–94).

While a number of formulas for preparing organic soilless mixes have been proposed, the two most widely used and accepted are the peat-lite[13] and the U.C. Mix formulas[14]. From these basic formulas, a number of related mixes for various uses have been devised. An ingredients list for some of these mixes is given in Table 14.

TABLE 14. INGREDIENTS TO MAKE ONE CUBIC YARD OF SOILLESS ORGANIC MIX

Ingredient	Cornell Peat-Lite*	U.C. Mix #D*	U.C. Mix #E*	Canada Mix Seedling*	NJ Tomato Greenhouse	Georgia Greenhouse Tomato
Sphagnum peatmoss	11 bu.	16.5 bu	22 bu.	12 bu.	9 bu.	—
Milled pinebark	—	—	—	—	—	9 bu.
Vermiculite	11 bu.	—	—	10 bu.	9 bu.	9 bu.
Perlite	—	—	—	—	4 bu.	—
Sand	—	5.5 bu.	—	—	—	—
Limestone	5 lbs.	9 lbs.	7.5 lbs.	4 lbs.	8 lbs.	10 lbs.
Superphosphate (0-20-0)	2 lbs.	2 lbs.	1 lb.	1 lb.	2 lbs.	—
5-10-5 fertilizer	6 lbs.	—	—	—	—	—
10-10-10 fertilizer	—	—	—	2 lbs.	—	10 lbs.
Potassium nitrate	—	—	0.3 lb.	0.5 lb.	—	—
Calcium nitrate	—	—	—	—	1 lb.	—
Magnesium sulfate	—	—	—	—	—	3 lbs.
Calcium sulfate	—	—	—	—	—	5 lbs.
Borax	10 gms.	—	—	1 gm.	10 gms.	—
Chelated Iron	25 gms.	—	—	—	35 gms.	—

*These mixes are mainly for shot-term growth, while the other mixes are for long-term greenhouse tomato.

13. J.W. Boodley and R. Sheldrake, Jr. 1954. Cornell Peat-Lite Mixes for Commerical Plant Growing. Cornell Extension Bulletin 1104.
14. K.F. Baker (ed). 1957. The U.C. System for Producing Healthy Container Grown Plants. University of California Division of Agricultural Science. Agr. Expt. Sta.

In addition to the grower-made mixes based on various formulas, there are a number of commercially prepared organic soilless mixes available for specific crops and uses which are usually designated by the manufacturer. Most of these mixes are various combinations of sphagnum peatmoss, pine bark and vermiculite. In some instances, the composition of the mix reflects more the cost and availability of the major materials than the physical and chemical characteristics they give to the mix. For example, the increased cost and reduced availability of sphagnum peatmoss has led to substitution with other materials. Pine bark has been a common substitute.

Composts of various kinds, such as course sawdust, composted garbage and other organic refuse, and sewage sludges, have been added to mixes. The relatively low cost and the need for disposal have lead to the introduction of these composted materials into some organic soilless mixes. Unfortunately, some composts contain heavy metal residues. These elements, if present in high concentrations, are toxic to plants. Cadmium (Cd), chromium (Cr), copper (Cu), lead (Pb), manganese (Mn), and zinc (Zn) are common elements found in garbage and sewage composts. While these composts can be treated to reduce heavy metal concentrations to below levels toxic to plants, their use should be limited to the growing of non-edible crops.

Particle size and distribution in a soilless organic mix is as important as its chemical composition. Finess determines whether a mix is best suited for short-or long-term use. In a FINE mix, the majority of its particles are less than 0.59 millimeters in diameter and will pass a NBS sieve number 20. The majority of the particles in a COURSE mix will not pass a NBS sieve number 8, being 2.38 millimeters or larger in diameter.

Particle size distribution is an important consideration in organic soilless media culture since it determines both water holding capacity and aeration of the mix. High water holding capacity and humid air spaces in the mix are important for germination, and seedling and cutting growth; while good aeration and moderate water holding capacity are essential for long-term plantings. A FINE particle mix is best for seed germination and short-term plant production of seedlings and cuttings; the COURSE mixes are best for long-term use, such as growing potted flowering and woody ornamental plants.

For container growing long term, the percentage of particles less than 0.59 millimeters in size should not exceed 20 to 30 per cent to minimize water logging. On the other hand, for short term use, the course particles of 2.38 millimeters or larger should be completely removed from the mix.

In general, mixtures of sphagnum peatmoss and vermiculite and/or perlite make up a majority of the FINE organic mixtures, while pine bark alone or with perlite constitute most of the COURSE mixes. However, this is a generalization that does not entirely hold for all mix types as pine bark can be processed to make as fine a mix as sphagnum peatmoss.

A common component added to organic mixes is sand. It is used to alter either the water holding capacity and/or weight of the mix. Sand is added to provide porosity in FINE mixes or when weight is needed to keep plant containers upright in either FINE or COURSE mixes. Sand should not constitute more than 20 to 25 per cent of the mix. If more than 50 per cent of a mix is sand, weight becomes a problem. The recommended grade of sand is "builders" sand which is a course particle sand, all passing a 10-mesh sieve but only 30% a 40-mesh sieve.

Segregation will occur during the preparation and handling of an organic soilless mix since the components (sphagnum peatmoss, pine bark, perlite, vermiculite, sand, etc.) vary in particle size and density. Therefore, care is required when preparing, mixing and handling to prevent segregation. This is particularly important when fertilizer ingredients are being blended into a mix. Even in an automatic potting machine, an organic soilless mix may be segregated as it is moved from the mixing bin to the pot filling chute. Making or keeping the mix slightly moist during handling and mixing helps keep components from easily segregating.

Segregation of components is a common problem in prepared mixes due to separation during shipment, as the less dense and larger particles move upward through the mix. Upon receipt and prior to use, careful turning of the mix is required to restore the materials to their original blend.

Normally, the essential elements are added to the organic soilless mix prior to use. The mix formulas detailed in Table 14 list some of the common fertilizer substances added. Slow-release fertilizers are frequently added for elemental control in the mix. Ureaform[15], Osmocote[16], MagAmp[17], and ordinary chemical-based fertilizer placed in small perforated polyethylene bags placed in the mix, give some degree of control of elemental release to provide a steady supply of essential elements during the growing season as well as reducing leaching losses. However, the high cost of commonly prepared slow-release fertilizers must be balanced against the advantages of control and use.

Limestone has traditionally been added to organic soilless mixes (see Table 14), both to raise the water pH of the mix and as a source of calcium (Ca) and magnesium (Mg). However, recent research raises questions about this practice, since raising the pH of the mix, even moderately, can significantly reduce the availability of some essential elements (Figure 16).

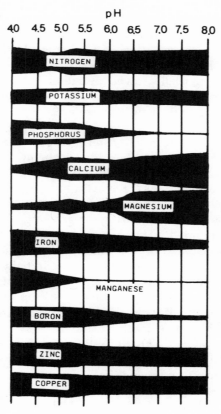

Figure 16. Availability of plant nutrients at different pH levels for W.R. Grace Metro Mix 300.

(from: John C. Peterson. 1982. Effects of pH upon Nutrient Availability in a Commerical Soilless Root Medium Utilized for Floral Crop Production. Ohio Agricultural Research Circular 268, pp 16–19, Ohio Agricultural Research & Development Center, Wooster.)

15. Hercules Powder Company, Wilmington, Delaware.
16. Sierra Chemical Company, Milpitas, California.
17. W.R. Grace Company, Baltimore, Maryland.

The maximum water pH for an organic soilless mix should not exceed 5.5, with the optimum range being between 5.0 and 5.5. Elimination of limestone from organic soilless mix formulas requires a substitute source for Ca, either as calcium sulfate ($CaSO_4$) or calcium nitrate [$Ca(NO_3)_2$]; and for Mg, magnesium sulfate ($MgSO_47H_2O$). Several formulas recommended by the author are given in Table 15.

TABLE 15. FORMULAS FOR PREPARING A PINE BARK SOILLESS MEDIUM WITH AND WITHOUT THE ADDITION OF AGRICULTURAL LIMESTONE

Lime and fertilizer materials	Pounds per cubic yard of pine bark	
	with Lime	without Lime
Limestone (dolomitic)	10	none
10-10-10 fertilizer	10	10
Calcium sulfate	5	15
Magnesium sulfate	3	9

Irrigation water alters the pH of an organic soilless mix if the water contains sizeable quantities of either Ca or Mg, or both. With each irrigation, the mix is essentially "limed," and the water pH of the mix raises a bit. In time, the pH reaches the point where the availability of some of the essential elements is adversely affected and plant deficiencies occur. The problem can be partially solved by either not adding Ca or Mg containing fertilizers to the mix, thereby relying on the Ca and Mg in the irrigation water to provide the crop requirement, or treating the irrigation water to remove its Ca and Mg content (see page 36).

From a practical standpoint and for short-term cropping (a growth period of less than eight weeks), the essential elements may be added to the mix when constituted. However, from a control standpoint, and for all long-term cropping, adding the essential elements as required is best. If the grower decides for practical reasons to add some of the elements when constituting the mix, it is wisest to incorporate only the micronutrients, reserving the major elements for addition as needed during the growing season. Unfortunately, no one best way can be recommended. The best compromise between considerations of practicality and control appears to be the adding of the micronutrients and the major elements P, Ca and Mg to the organic soilless mix initially, and then supplement as required based either on plant and mix tests or growth and plant appearance, and to add the major elements N and K periodically to satisfy the crop requirement based on growth and plant appearance. The element P may be added to the latter group if a complete NPK fertilizer is usded to supply the required N and K.

Liquid fertilizer, such as the 20–20–20 (N-P_2O_5-K_2O), is frequently used for supplementation by adding to the irrigation water. The concentration is varied slightly depending on the crop requirement. Most recommend that the concentration be such that the nitrogen (N) concentration be between 50- and 100-parts per million (ppm). A list of materials and the amount required to prepare 50-, 100-, 150-, and 200-ppm N fertilizer solutions is given in Table 16.

Growers should be aware that repeated long-term use of a fertilizer such as 20–20–20 can lead to excesses in phosphorus (P) if this element has been already added to the mix. Therefore, care should be taken to ensure that P excess does not occur by not putting P into the mix initially or by selecting a liquid fertilizer that does not contain the element P.

A combination recommended for tomatoes and other vegetable crops is an equal quantity of calcium and potassium nitrates [$Ca(NO_3)_2$ and KNO_3] with 50 ppm nitrate being supplied by each salt. Potassium nitrate (KNO_3) alone is sufficient if all the other major elements have already been added to the mix.

TABLE 16. POUNDS OF FERTILIZER PER 100 GALLONS OF WATER TO MAKE 50-, 100-, 150-, AND 200-PPM NITROGEN SOLUTION FOR FERTILIZER SUPPLEMENTATION

Fertilizer	lbs per 100 gallons water			
	50	100	150	200 ppm N
calcium nitrate	0.24	0.48	0.72	0.96
potassium nitrate	0.32	0.64	0.96	1.28
5-10-5	0.83	1.66	2.49	3.32
10-10-10	0.41	0.83	1.29	1.66
20-20-20	0.20	0.41	0.63	0.83

At this point, the reader may be confused as to the proper constitution and use of an organic soilless mix and, indeed, this confusion is wide spread. There are no set rules. There is considerable literature on the use of organic soilless mixes for plant production with little uniformity as to technique of growing. It is evident that for short-term growing, a wide range of conditions can be tolerated in terms of mix constituents and methods of fertilization. Grower's observation and experience is the primary control. By adding or withholding fertilizer, the rate of growth and plant appearance can be easily changed. It is when an organic soilless mix is used for long-term growing that mix constituents and fertilization technique become critical. Many of the problems occurring in other forms of soilless and hydroponic growing appear, such as, soluble salt accumulation, disease control, pH shifts, and nutrient element stress. Only by both observation and testing that the grower can control these factors to prevent reduction in plant growth and yield.

There is considerable literature on the use of organic soilless mixes for plant production and it would be impossible to summarize all of it. In 1980, the proceedings of a symposium on the use of organic substrates for plant growing was published[18]. Topics included the use of various organic substances, methods of fertilization and nutrient element control. A recent bibliography[19] on the horticultural uses of bark provides a listing of past and current literature of interest to the organic soilless mix grower.

It would be useful to describe a few of the more unique applications of organic soilless mixes for long-term growing, rather than attempting to describe all possible applications. In this way, comparisons can be made between the use of organic soilless mixes and other soilless growing techniques.

Traditional organic soilless media culture is carried out with the medium placed in either a bed, pot or can. Water, with or without fertilizer added, is dripped into the container in quantities relative to the atmospheric demand on the plant. As in the case of gravel and sand systems, the medium must be flushed with water periodically to remove accumulated salts. The need to flush is determined by the soluble salt readings of the effluent from the container. Commonly, the container is discarded after one use, although some growers have devised interesting schemes to use the medium for more than one crop; for example, growing a crop of tomatoes followed by an outdoor ornamental tree or shrub[20]. The sale of the ornamental plant also provides a means of disposing of the container and media—and at a profit!

Another popular growing technique is to plant directly into the medium shipping bag

18. G.S. Wilson (Ed). 1980. Symposium on Substances in Horticulture Other than Soils in Situ. ACTA HORTICULTURAE No. 99. The Hague, The Netherlands.
19. Frank Pokorny. 1982. Horticultural Uses of Bark-Softwood and Hardwood: A Bibliography. Georgia Agricultural Experiment Station Research Report 402. Athens, Georgia 30602.
20. Tim D. Carpenter. 1979. Containerized Growing Systems for Greenhouse Vegetables. pp 1–20. IN Proceedings Hydroponics: The Soilless Alternative. Hydroponic Society of America, Brentwood, California 94513. USA.

(see Figure 10) of mix, adding the required essential elements and water by drip irrigation. Normally, the mix is supplemented with micronutrients (see Table 14) and the major elements applied in a nutrient solution whose composition is comparable to a Hoagland's nutrient solution without micronutrients (see Table 6). The flow of the nutrient solution through the drip irrigation system is sufficient to meet the water requirement. If plant growth is normal, elemental utilization should be sufficient to prevent a significant accumulation of excess salts. When plant growth is slow due to poor external growing conditions, then applying only water without elements added is best, resuming the nutrient solution application when growth conditions improve. Some growers substitute a mixture of an equal ratio of potassium and calcium nitrate [KNO_3 and $Ca(NO_3)_2$] to give a solution containing 100 ppm nitrogen (N) in place of the Hoagland formula. If this is done, then the medium must contain sufficient phosphorus (P) and magnesium (Mg) to meet the crop requirement (see Table 14).

The most unique application of an organic soilless mix is in a system employing subirrigation, based on a technique first introduced by Geraldson[21] in 1963, for the growing of staked tomatoes in the sandy soils of southwestern Florida. In fields where the water table level can be controlled, raised plastic covered beds are prepared with a band of fertilizer placed down each side of the bed. Tomato plants are set in the center of the beds and the roots grow into that area of the soil which is balanced in its water and elemental content (see Figure 17). The same system can be duplicated by placing a COURSE organic soilless mix into a watertight box so that a constant water table can be maintained under the mix.

A $4' \times 30' (1 \times 9m)$ grow-box system, employing an equal volume mixture of pine bark and vermiculite as the growing medium supplemented with limestone and fertilizer as shown in the last column of Table 14, was successfully used to grow greenhouse tomatoes, cucumbers and snapdragons over a 8 year period[22] (Figure 18). A constant water table is maintained

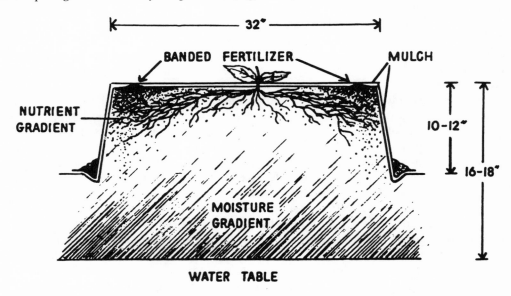

Figure 17. Control of the root ionic environment obtained by banding fertilizer on the surface of a raised bed, using a mulch cover and maintaining a definite water table.

21. C.M. Geraldson. 1963. Quantity and Balance of Nutrients Required for Best Yields and Quality of Tomatoes. Proceedings Florida State Horticultural Society 76: 153–158.
22. R.R. Bruce, J.E. Pallas, L.A. Harper and J.B. Jones. 1980. Water and Nutrient Element Regulation Prescription in Nonsoil Media for Greenhouse Crop Production. COMMUNICATIONS IN SOIL SCIENCE AND PLANT ANALYSIS 11(7): 677–698.

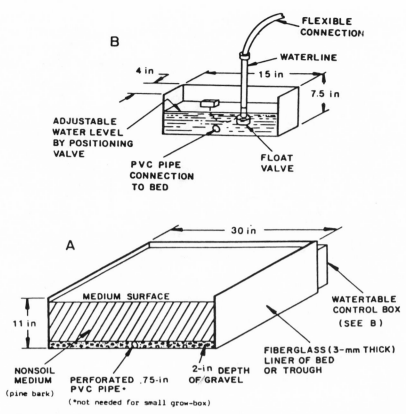

Figure 18. Pine bark grow-box system employing constant water table with automatic water level control.

under 7-inches (18 cm) of the growing medium with an automatic float value system. No water is applied overhead. Fertilizer is added to the medium between crops based on a test of the medium (see pages 151–153). The tomato crop is supplemented periodically with a mixture of KNO_3 and $Ca(NO_3)_2$ at 100 ppm N concentration based on need determined by plant physical appearance and plant analyses (see pages 88–92).

The pine bark-vermiculite mix maintained its physical characteristics over the 8 year period of use, requiring only small yearly additions of fresh material to maintain the initial volume. Initially, some boxes were filled with a FINE peat-lite mix which failed to maintain a good physical character beyond the first year and was discarded.

The success of this sub-irrigation grow-box system is due in large part to the constantly maintained water table which allows the roots to grow into that portion of the medium "ideal" in terms of water and elemental contents. The grower does not need to be concerned about watering on high atmospheric demand days as water is always available to the plant. As the growing system is almost self-regulating, the grower can concentrate his attention on other things.

The grow-box can be made in almost any size to accommodate a wide range of uses, even for outdoor family vegetable gardening[23]. The only critical dimension is the depth of the organic soilless medium which must be no more or less than 7 inches above the water table. The medium of COURSE pine bark seems to be the best of all the organic substances.

A similar system is the Skaife Method, first introduced as the PIPE DREAM[24]. Using

23. Jones, Jr., J.B. 1980. Construct Your Own Automatic Growing Machine. POPULAR SCIENCE 216(3): 87.
24. W. Troxell, E. Holcomb and E. Bergman. 1981. Hydroponics: Not Just a Pipe Dream. AMERICAN VEGETABLE GROWER 29(2): 28–29.

Figure 19. Skaife Pipe Dream with plastic mesh socks containing rooting medium with the sock reaching into the flow of nutrient solution in the horizontal pipe.

plastic sewer pipe, vertical pipe sections are inserted into a horizontal pipe containing a constant flowing nutrient solution. A COURSE peat is placed into a plastic mesh sock which fits into the vertical stand pipe, the base of the sock reaching into the flowing nutrient solution (Figure 19). Plants can be easily moved from one pipe to another without damaging the roots, making plant portability a significant advantage. From more recent research and experience, a modified system has been developed in which plant portability has been retained, but the design of the growing system is more like the grow-box described above.

The plastic mesh sock containing peat is still used as the growing medium. These are placed in vertical PVC pipes that have a number of 1" holes in them and are set in a large bed of a COURSE peat-lite mix over a constant water table. Roots can grow out of the sock into the larger bed. Portability is still retained as the sock can be lifted from the vertical tube with minimum root damage. This growing system, the Skaife Truck Farm, is to be marketed in a range sizes for home and commercial use[25].

D. CRITERIA FOR SOILLESS MEDIA CULTURE

It is obvious from the discussion of the various techniques for soilless media culture that some of these methods leave much to be desired. CLOSED systems that recirculate the nutrient solution can be particularly troublesome due to the changing composition of the nutrient solution with each use, the build-up of elements left behind in the rooting media and the potential for quickly spreading disease throughout the entire growing system from a single point of entry. Therefore, those systems that are OPEN, that is, those in which the nutrient solution is not recirculated, have a very distinct advantage.

But OPEN systems are not without difficulties. Substantial waste of water and elements not used by the crop are common. A build-up of elements can occur in the rooting media as

25. Skaife Truck Farm 1982. Skaife Method Incorporated, 4901 El Camino Real, Carlsbad, California 92008.

occurs in CLOSED systems. But, the two major advantages obtained with the OPEN system, nutrient solution composition and disease control, are sufficient to offset the waste of water and essential elements. By scheduling periodic leaching of the rooting media with pure water, the build-up of accumulated elements in the rooting media can be minimized in both systems.

The most common of all OPEN systems in wide use today is the drip-irrigation system. As described earlier (page 55), drip irrigation is rapidly becoming a major method of water and elemental control for a variety of growing situations.

Gravel and sand media growing systems are being phased out as growers turn either to the use of an organic soilless mix placed in individual containers or to an entirely medium-free system, such as the Nutrient Film Technique (NFT). Much of this shift reflects the desire on the part of the grower to better control his growing system.

The most promising organic soilless growing system is the sub-irrigation grow-box. All of the essential elements can be added to the organic medium, and in most cases, in sufficient quantity to satisfy the crop requirement for the entire growing season. By maintaining a constant water table under the organic medium, the crop is supplied with sufficient water to meet demand under all circumstances. Thus this system requires a minimum of effort on the part of the grower, providing the time needed by the grower to concentrate on managing the crop itself.

Chapter IX: Hydroponic Systems

According to the classification system devised by Larsen (see Figure 9), true hydroponics is the growing of plants in nutrient solution without a rooting medium. Plant roots are either suspended in standing aerated nutrient solution or the solution flows around the suspended roots. This definition is quiet different from the usually accepted concept of hydroponics which has in the past included all forms of soilless growing. Under the Larsen classification system, the only commercial application in use today that can properly be classified as HYDROPONICS is the Nutrient Film Technique (NFT) developed by Allen Cooper[7].

A. AERATED STANDING NUTRIENT SOLUTION

This is the oldest soilless culture technique dating back to the early researchers who, in the mid 1800s, used the technique to determine which elements were essential for plants. Sachs (1840) grew plants in aerated solutions, observing the effect on plant growth with the addition of various substances to the solution. This technique is still of use in various types of plant nutrition studies, although most researchers have turned to flowing and continuous replenishment nutrient solution procedures[26].

The essential requirements for the aerated standing nutrient solution technique are a suitable vessel, the nutrient solution and an air tube which bubbles air continuously into the nutrient solution as shown in Figure 20. The bubbling air serves to both add oxygen (O_2) to the nutrient solution and stir it. Depending on the size of the plant and volume of nutrient solution, the solution is replaced on a 7 to 14 day schedule. Water loss from the solution is replaced daily, usually with pure water. The commonly used formula is Hoagland's (see Table 6) or some modification of it. The plant/nutrient solution volume ratio should be 1 plant per 2 to 4 gallons (9 to 18 liters) of solution.

The best current description of an aerated standing nutrient solution system is given by Clark[27]. This technique is being used for studies on the elemental requirements of corn and sorghum. Several plants are grown in ½ gallon (2 liters) of nutrient solution with change schedules varying from 7 to 30 days depending on the stage of growth and plant species. The ratio of nitrate (NO_3^-) to ammonium (NH_4) in the nutrient solution is used to control the pH, the ratio normally being 8 to 1 with a total of 300 ppm N in solution. Clark's nutrient solution formula is given in Table 17.

Although Clark's technique is primarily designed for corn and sorghum nutritional studies, his method of nutrient solution management could be applied to other plant species.

This method of hydroponic growing is limited in its commercial applications, although lettuce has been successfully grown on styrofoam sheets floating on aerated nutrient solution. The plants are set in small holes in the styrofoam with their roots growing into the nutrient solution. The sheets are lifted from the solution when the plants are ready to harvest.

26. J.B. Jones, Jr. 1982. Hydroponics: Its History and Use in Plant Nutrition Studies. JOURNAL OF PLANT NUTRITION 5(8): 1003–1030.
27. R.B. Clark. 1982. Nutrient Solution Growth of Sorghum and Corn in Mineral Nutrition Studies. JOURNAL OF PLANT NUTRITION 5(8): 1039–1057.

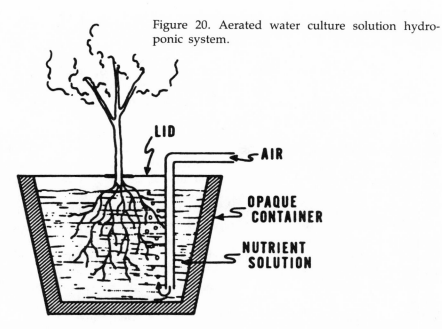

Figure 20. Aerated water culture solution hydroponic system.

TABLE 17. COMPOSITION OF NUTRIENT SOLUTION USED FOR THE GROWTH OF SORGHUM PLANTS

Solution number[†]	Salt	Stock solution Concn.	Stock soln. used	Cation		Anion		Final composition element	mg/liter	μM
		g/liter	ml/liter	.... mg element/liter				element	mg/liter	μM
1	$Ca(NO_3)_2 \cdot 4H_2O$	270.0	6.6	Ca	= 302.4	NO_3-N	= 211.4	Ca	302	7540
	NH_4NO_3	33.8		NH_4-N	= 39.0	NO_3-N	= 39.0	K	283	7240
								Mg	37.8	1550
								NO_3-N	321	22900
2	KCl	18.6	7.2	K	= 70.2	Cl	= 63.7	NH_4-N	39.0	2780
	K_2SO_4	44.6		K	= 142.2	S	= 58.3	Cl §	65.0	1940
	KNO_3	24.6		K	= 68.5	NO_3-N	= 24.5	S	58.5	1820
								P	2.00	65
3	$Mg(NO_3)_2 \cdot 6H_2O$	142.4	2.8	Mg	= 37.8	NO_3-N	= 43.6	Fe	2.76	49
								Mn	0.974	18
4	KH_2PO_4	17.6	0.5	K	= 2.5	P	= 2.00	B	0.536	50
								Zn	0.300	4.6
5‡	$Fe(NO_3)_3 \cdot 9H_2O$	13.31	1.5	Fe	= 2.76	NO_3-N	= 2.1	Cu	0.076	1.2
	HEDTA	8.68		Na	= 4.48§	HEDTA	= 13.0	Mo	0.155	1.6
								Na §	4.56	200
6	$MnCl_2 \cdot 4H_2O$	2.34	1.5	Mn	= 0.974	Cl	= 1.3	HEDTA	13.0	47
	H_3BO_3	2.04				B	= 0.536			
	$ZnSO_4 \cdot 7H_2O$	0.88		Zn	= 0.300	S	= 0.147			
	$CuSO_4 \cdot 5H_2O$	0.20		Cu	= 0.076	S	= 0.038			
	$Na_2MoO_4 \cdot 2H_2O$	0.26		Na	= 0.074	Mo	= 0.155			

† In each solution the respective salts were dissolved together in the same volume. Some of the salts in solutions 1 to 4 may be combined to make fewer stock solutions if desired, but keep Ca salts separate from SO_4 and PO_4 salts. Combinations of the salts noted are for convenience.

‡ This solution was prepared by (a) dissolving the HEDTA [N-2-(hydroxyethyl)-ethylenediaminetriacetaic acid] in 200 ml distilled water + 80 ml. IN NaOH; (b) adding solid $Fe(NO_3)_3 \cdot 9H_2O$ to the HEDTA solution and completely dissolving the Fe salt; (C) adjusting the pH to 4.0 with small additions of IN NaOH (approx. 50 ml); and, (d) bringing the solution to volume. Care should be taken not to add NaOH in step (c) too rapidly to allow Fe to precipitate. The HEDTA was obtained from Aldrich Chemical Co., Milwaukee, WI (catalog No. H2650-2). This source of HEDTA is not the only source available and mention of this company or product does not constitute a guarantee or warranty of the company or product by the U.S. Department of Agriculture and does not imply the product approval to the exclusion of others that may be suitable.

§ Assumes 130 ml IN NaOH used to adjust pH of FeHEDTA to 4.0 and no pH adjustment of nutrient solution.

B. NUTRIENT FILM TECHNIQUE (NFT)

The latest and most significant development in hydroponics today is Dr. Allen Cooper's NUTRIENT FILM TECHNIQUE, frequently referred to as NFT[7]. Some have modified the name by using the word FLOW in place of FILM, since the plant roots are indeed growing in a flow of nutrient solution.

Plant roots are suspended in a trough or channel through which the nutrient solution passes as shown in Figure 21. Being a CLOSED system, the nutrient solution is recycled in much the same manner as in gravel or sand bed-sump soilless media systems. Therefore, the difficulties associated with those systems can develop with NFT, except that there is no support medium which can absorb and retain elements from the nutrient solution.

The trough or channel containing the plant roots is set on a slope (usually about 1%) so that the nutrient solution can flow from the top to the lower end by gravity. Normally, the nutrient solution is introduced into the upper end of the trough at ¼ gallon (1 liter) per minute. As the root mat increases in size, the flow rate down the trough diminishes. Plants at the upper end of the trough may reduce the oxygen (O_2) and/or elemental content of the nutrient solution sufficiently to significantly affect the growth and development of plants at the lower end. Furthermore, as the root mat thickens and becomes more dense, the flowing nutrient solution tends to move over the top and down the outer edge of the mat, reducing its contact with the entire root system. This interruption in the flow results in poor mixing of the current flowing nutrient solution with water and elements left behind in the root mat from previous nutrient solution flows.

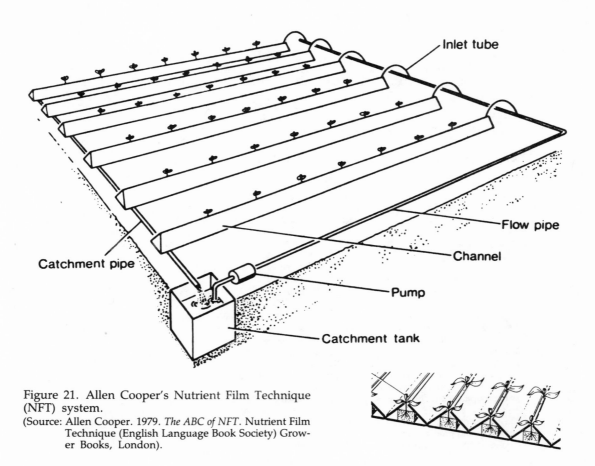

Figure 21. Allen Cooper's Nutrient Film Technique (NFT) system.
(Source: Allen Cooper. 1979. *The ABC of NFT*. Nutrient Film Technique (English Language Book Society) Grower Books, London).

In order to minimize these effects, the trough should be no longer than 30 feet in length and a minimum of 12 inches wide or wider, if possible. The channels are usually formed by folding a wide strip of polyethylene into a "pipe-like" trough. The polyethylene may be either white or black but must be opaque to keep light out. If light enters the trough, algae growth becomes a serious problem.

The plants are set in the trough at the spacing recommended for that crop. Usually, plants are started in germination cubes made of fiberglass or similar material. The cube with its started plant is set directly in the trough. The polyethylene sheet is pulled round the plant stem and closed with pins or clips, forming a light proof "pipe-like" rooting trough. Experience has shown that the germination cube should be of a substance other than peat or similar material that may disintegrate. A durable germination cube helps keep the plant set in place in the NFT trough.

Major advantages of NFT are the ease of establishment and the relative low cost of construction materials. Support for the trough can be inexpensively made of wood or sheet metal. The channel material, if made of strips of polyethylene, can be discarded after each crop, only necessitating sterilization of the permanent piping and nutrient solution storage tank.

Disease control can be difficult since a disease organism entering an NFT system will be quickly carried from one plant to another, and one trough to another. Therefore, the same precautions are required as with any CLOSED recirculating nutrient solution growing system. In warm climatic areas, the fungus disease—pythium, is the major organism affecting plants grown in NFT systems. Presently, there seems to be no legal method of controlling this organism, although temperature and the concentration of copper (Cu), and possibly manganese (Mn) and zinc (Zn) in the nutrient solution, as well as its pH, may be adjusted to offer some degree of control. However, current research and grower experience has not been sufficient to offer hope for effective pythium control using any of these modifications of the nutrient solution. Pythium does not seem to be a serious problem when the temperature of the nutrient solution is maintained at less then 77°F (25°C).

"Root-death" is another problem in NFT installations. Recently, it has been suggested that concern is greater than justified, in-as-much as "root-death" is a natural physiological phenomenon brought on by competition within the plant for carbohydrates. During periods of high demand for carbohydrates (primarily at fruiting or during times of stress), some roots will die. But when stress is relieved, plant tissue regains an adequate carbohydrate supply and new roots will appear. As long as most of the roots in the mat are white in color, little attention should be paid to "root-death." This phenomenon probably occurs in all systems of growing but is clearly visible in NFT and not so easily seen when roots are growing in a media.

The nutrient solution formula as given by Cooper (see Table 12), or slight modifications of it, are generally used by NFT growers.

It is common practice to use half-strength formula for the make-up water to replace that lost by transpiration. The formula for NFT growing of tomato and cucumber is given in Table 13 (see page 95). It is varied to reflect both stages of growth and plant species. The make-up formula (or topping-up solution as it is called) for this modification is also specified.

Normally, the nutrient solution is monitored by periodic conductivity-measurements which determines the appropriate times to add make-up (or topping-up) nutrient solution to maintain initial volume, and when to dump and make a new batch of nutrient solution. It is not common practice to monitor the composition of the nutrient solution by elemental analysis. In one commercial NFT system[28], the essential elements are injected into flowing stream of nutrient solution, based on either a conductivity measurement, or on expected elemental usage by the crop in production. Calcium nitrate [$Ca(NO_3)_2$] solution is injected

28. Hygroponics, Incorporated, 3935 North Palo Alto Ave., Panama City, Florida 32405. USA.

into the nutrient solution by some growers as a means of maintaining the proper conductivity level. pH may or may not be monitored and adjusted periodically. The suggested best pH range is between 6.0 and 7.0. Dilute nitric acid (HNO_3) is the usual reagent injected into the solution to lower the pH, and either amonium hydroxide (NH_4OH) or potassium hydroxide (KOH) to raise the pH.

A new practice which is gaining in use, is to intermittently flow the nutrient solution down the trough in an "on-off" cycle. Some have adopted a "half-on, half-off" circulation period, while others have developed a more sophisticated system, basing the timing of recirculation on accumulation of incoming radiation. When 0.3 millijoules per square meter (mJ/m^2) of light energy has accumulated, the nutrient solution is flowed down the trough for 30 minutes. Such systems have proven to be successful in producing better, and higher yielding tomato and cucumber crops.

The relative ease of controlling the temperature of the nutrient solution with NFT systems is an advantage, particularly for winter greenhouse vegetable production. With the nutrient solution temperature set at 82°F (28°C), there is a marked increase in water and elemental uptake. At this temperature, the optimum recommended night-time air temperature for the crop in the greenhouse can be reduced 5°F (3°C) with little effect on plant growth and yield. Such systems of temperature control and readjustment have as their objective increased energy efficiency by reduction in heating costs. Growers need to balance and growth benefits against the dangers of root disease problems that might appear at these elevated solution temperatures.

Equally important is control of the minimum temperature. When the nutrient solution temperature is less than 68°F (20°C), a marked affect on root growth occurs (see page 62). At low temperatures, there are fewer root laterials and the roots are course in appearance. Water and elemental uptake is slowed. Plants may begin to wilt on high atmospheric demand days and elemental deficiencies appear. Therefore, care must be taken to insure that the nutrient solution temperature is kept above this minimum.

In 1979, a SYMPOSIUM ON RESEARCH ON RECIRCULATING CULTURE[29] was held. Topics included physiological, nutritional, horticultural and pathological aspects of recirculating water culture systems, including NFT. Little practical information was presented, the main focus of the Symposium being research on how plants respond to various environments created by the technique. The nature and tone of the remarks made in some papers are not encouraging to those looking to NFT as the "Ideal" technique for hydroponic growing. Oxygen (O_2) depletion and elemental control of the nutrient solution loom as major problems with the system.

Seven Symposium papers dealt with disease control, pointing to the difficulties encountered by growers attempting to control infestations in a CLOSED recirculating water culture system. There were 15 papers on nutrient solution formulas and essential element control as well as other research reported, topics that have been discussed in some detail in this book. However, the Symposium proceedings are useful reading for growers trying to obtain a better feel for the current state of the NFT art.

There are several manufacturers of NFT systems in the United States, Hydroponics, Incorporated[28] being one of the major suppliers of such systems. Their units for growing lettuce and cucumbers are shown in Figures 22 and 23, respectively, to give the reader an overview of the layout.

As advantage of the NFT growing system is the ability of the grower to use a variety of configurations in the design of the rooting trough, as long as there is ample room for root growth. One unique system uses a large tube hung by cable attached to movable posts so that the row spacing can be changed as the plant increases in size. The cable-attached tube sags in the middle so the nutrient solution is introduced at either end and collected for

29. R.G. Hurd (Ed). 1980. Symposium on Research on Recirculating Water Culture. ACTA HORTICULTURAE No. 98. The Hague, Netherlands.

Figure 22. Lettuce (European Bibb-Ostinata) growing in the Hygro-Trough® lettuce system. The troughs are spaced 6″ on center and the plants are spaced 6″ apart in the troughs. The valve in the foreground controls the rate of flow to eleven troughs which are fed through holes in the PVC pipe running above them. The troughs slope toward the side of the greenhouse *(background)* where they drain into a return gutter which feeds back into the reservoir. The younger plants have been in the troughs for about a week. The older plants have been in the troughs for about four weeks and are ready to be harvested.

Source: Hygroponics, Inc., Panama City, Florida.
J.W. Brown.

Figure 23. Pre-fruiting European cucumber plants growing in the Hygro-Flo® system. The plant roots are in the black plastic Hygro-Flo tube which has been painted white to reflect light and help reduce heat buildup in the nutrient solution circulating through the tubes. The grow tables which hold the Hygro-Flo tubes are given a 1½% slope by the headers of decreasing height upon which they rest. The Dike Stick® which passes through the Hygro-Flo tube mid-way between two plants holds the plastic tube up allowing a blanket of air to exist over the wet root mat. The painted wood under the tables covers the nutrient reservoir. The nutrient solution is pumped from the reservoir to the Hygro-Flo tubes from which it drains into return lines leading back into the reservoir. The cement floors are painted white to reflect light. They are easy to keep clean and help reduce the problem with insects and fungus diseases.

Source: Hygroponics, Inc., Panama City, Florida.
J.W. Brown

Figure 24. Modified NFT system with sand filled styrofoam cups set in access holes of PVC pipe containing a flow of nutrient solution.

(Source: Normandy Technologies, P.O. Box 13560, St. Louis, Missouri 13560.)

reuse at the mid point. The object here is to better utilize greenhouse space over the growing season by adjusting row width.

The NFT principle has been applied to smaller growing units for home garden use. One such application for vegetable growing places sand-filled styrofoam cups in access holes in PVC pipes[30]. Nutrient solution is circulated through the pipe on a timed schedule. This system has the unique feature of easy removal of plants from the system just by lifting the styroform cup from its access hole. A typical arrangement for this home garden NFT system is shown in Figure 24.

When Allen Cooper first introduced his NFT system of hydroponic growing, it was heralded as the hydroponic system of the future. It was, indeed, the first major change in hydroponic growing to be introduced since the 1930s. But, experience has shown that NFT does not solve the common problems inherent in most soilless and hydroponic growing systems. However, this did not deter its rapid acceptance and use in many parts of the world, particularly in Western Europe and England. NFT is still the most widely talked about and tested hydroponic system yet devised. But its future is highly questionable unless better means of disease and nutrient solution control are found.

C. AEROPONICS

Probably the most promising hydroponic technique of the future is aeroponics which is the distribution of water and essential elements by means of an aerosol mist bathing the plant roots as shown in Figure 25. The system is designed to achieve substantial economies is the use of both water and essential elements. The critical aspects of the technique are the character of the aerosol, frequency of root exposure and composition of the nutrient solution.

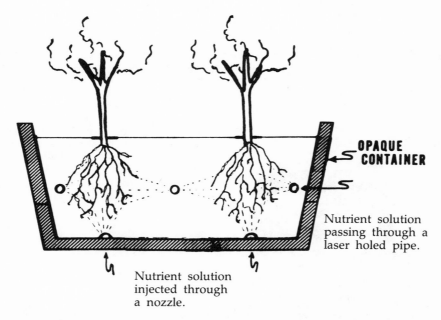

Figure 25. Aeroponic system of growing plants hydroponically showing two different methods of injecting the nutrient mist.

30. Family Food Garden. Normandy Technologies, P.O. Box 13560, St. Louis, Missouri 63138.

Several methods have been tried employing a spray of the nutrient solution rather than a fine mist. If this method of distributing the nutrient solution is used, droplet size and the frequency of exposure of the roots to the nutrient solution are critical factors in the technique. Continuous exposure to a fine mist may give better results than intermittent spraying or misting. However, the details of the application of the nutrient solution have yet to be fully determined.

One of the major advantages of the technique as compared to flowing the nutrient solution past the plant roots is aeration, since the roots are essentially growing in air.

One can conceive of a one-way passage of the nutrient solution with relatively low water use. With a carefully controlled balance between atmospheric demand and the intensity of the mist, economies in water and elemental use could be maximized. There are no large scale aeroponic systems as yet on the market, although this might change in the near future.

In Israel, Adi Limited[31] has announced an aeroponic system which they say has proved to be highly successful. The system is computer controlled and requires a special fogging device, troughs and an array of sensing devices. Although yields of crops obtained with this growing system have been reported to be considerably above those obtained with conventional hydroponic systems, the initial cost for the Adi system is very high, bringing into question its commercial viability.

It could be that the need for special devices and computer control will limit the future for aeroponics due to high initial and operating costs. However, if there are substantial yield capabilities obtainable with these aeroponic systems, costs may be quickly offset.

The best nutrient solution formula for an aeroponic system has not been determined, although beginning with a Hoagland's (see Table 6) solution would probably be a good starting point. Full strength nutrient solution would be required for intermittent large droplet sized droplet systems. With increased frequency of root misting and reduced droplet size, half-or-less strength solution might be sufficient. If the aeroponic system is operated as a CLOSED system, then the same factors affecting any CLOSED system must be dealt with. However, aeroponics offers the best opportunity to take advantage of an OPEN system, and at the same time, minimize the waste of water and essential elements inherent in most OPEN systems.

Aeroponics, as a method for growing hydroponically, has considerable potential and could be the hydroponic technique of the future. Although, its unique ability to precisely control the rooting environment is scientifically sound, commercial application may be limited by high costs.

D. DEVISING THE IDEAL SYSTEM

Unfortunately, the IDEAL hydroponic system has yet to be devised. However, the characteristics of an ideal system can at least be defined, the direct outcome of experience with the shortcomings of current systems. The primary objective of this exercise is to conceive of a system that is both commercially feasible, and highly productive in terms of plant growth and yield.

It is far easier to describe those characteristics which must be avoided than those that would make the system IDEAL. It is quite obvious that CLOSED systems which recirculate the nutrient solution are not desirable since recirculation can spread disease and other undesirable organisms very rapidly. In addition, nutrient solution composition changes with each use, unless expensive and difficult-to-manage procedures are invoked to re-constitute it after each pass through the growing media or rooting vessel.

31. Aeroponics in Israel. 1982. HORTSCIENCE 17(2): 137.

It is obviously wise to avoid systems requiring sizeable quantities of water. Even more importantly, systems which require the periodic discarding of large quantities of nutrient solution must be avoided. Such practices are costly both in the use of water and essential elements.

The question of the value and function of a root supporting media must be considered also. It has been noted that gravel and sand bed systems are difficult to manage from a number of standpoints. Elemental build-up and sterilization are two major problems. Other types of rooting media, both inorganic and organic, have their own shortcomings. Personal experience suggests that perlite and pine bark are probably the best of the presently used media, given that the grower must make the best of a less-than-ideal situation. There are good reasons for avoiding the use of any rooting media whatsoever, since the accumulation of elements in the media must be dealt with and can be difficult to control.

Most soilless culture and hydroponic systems require delivery of the nutrient solution by means of pumps, tubing, pipes, drippers, etc., all of which require constant attention. Those systems that move large quantities of nutrient solution periodically require a good deal of energy. So, it is obvious that the IDEAL soilless growing system should not require the moving of large quantities of nutrient solution in short periods of time. On the other hand, the presently available low water-use systems—drip, trickle, etc.—require an inordinate amount of attention to keep the system operable. Despite the introduction of elaborate filtering systems (with their attendant high maintenance costs), the extensive array of fine distribution piping and emitters seem to plug easily and frequently.

It would seem that we are describing a perpetual motion machine, an impossibility, for our IDEAL hydroponic system. The challange is to incorporate into this IDEAL system those features which out of years of experience have proved that they will yield maximum utilization of water and the essential elements; no moving parts; low cost; and high productivity in terms of plant growth and yield. Therefore, the IDEAL hydroponic system is one in which plant roots are suspended in a constant composition environment of water and essential elements, adequately aerated and sufficient in size to accommodate root growth. The key rests with what is needed to establish and manage a constant composition environment.

The future for soilless culture will be bright, indeed, if systems more efficient and better controlled than now in current use are developed. Certainly the most promising technique for hydroponic growing is aeroponics, and for soilless medium growing, the constant water table procedure using perlite or some similar material as the rooting medium. Breakthroughs in our understanding of plant growth and development will significantly add to developments that will come in hydroponic and soilless media growing. Vast improvements in both systems will be needed to make either system economically feasible for use in the future.

Chapter X: Pest Control

There is nothing unique about soilless or hydroponic growing with respect to pest control. The same procedures as used in growing in soil must be practiced to avoid disease and insect problems. In fact, control measures are more important for the hydroponic grower as the nutrient solution can be an ideal environment for some types of pests unless measures are taken to keep them out.

In most instances, good pest control is based on common sense—keeping growing and working areas clean, and using good sanitation practices. Keeping pests out of a crop is easier than attempting to control them after they have made their appearance. The trend today is away from chemical control, if at all possible. Since pest control is highly specific depending on the crop and method of growing, only general recommendations can be given in this text. However, general recommendations can go a long way in preventing the occurrence of a pest problem, thereby avoiding the hazards of a lost crop or the expense of continuous chemical usage.

Sanitation is by far the most important pest control procedure one can adopt. Since most pest problems are "brought to" the crop, preventing their entrance lies at the root of a good pest management program. Prevention includes using "clean" or sterilized containers, plants, water, growth media, etc. It means keeping the growing area free of foreign plants. Tools, equipment and materials (including clothing), hands and footware, must be kept free of disease organisms. The vast majority of pest problems are preventable if such procedures become routine practice.

Prevention by the use of chemicals is equally important when dealing with pest problems known to be of common occurrence. For example, it is always good practice to keep plants "covered" with a fungicide to prevent commonly occurring fungus diseases from gaining a foothold. Maintaining specific spray or fumigation schedules are also good practices inorder to keep insect populations under control. Waiting until there are signs of disease or insect pressures may be too late to regain the upper hand. An equally common practice is to vary the type of chemicals applied to prevent the development of pest immunity.

The nutrient solution is an ideal environment for the growth of algae and other pests. Minimizing exposure of the nutrient solution to light can prevent the growth of algae which, if given a foothold in the nutrient solution, will clog delivery tubes, pipes and valves. Filters of various kinds (see page 69) can remove suspended substances from the nutrient solution. Millipore[3] filtering will, to some extent remove some disease producing organisms from the solution. Some pest control chemicals can be added to the nutrient solution to control disease; however, great care is required to keep the concentration at levels that will provide pest control but not harm the crop.

The kinds of pest problems a grower may confront and their control, varies considerably from one geographic area to another. It is essential that the grower become familiar with these specific pests and recommended control measures. The recommended chemicals should be on hand and application equipment readied for use at the first sign of a pest or disease problem which may have economic consequences if not quickly brought under control. Daily monitoring procedures must be developed and routinely practiced. It is important to be familiar with those levels of pest incidence considering damaging and economically important to control. Every grower must be able to recognize at what level a pest can be tolerated, therefore, requiring no treatment.

A pest problem must be properly identified before any corrective step is taken. In certain cases, it may be necessary to call on a trained expert to assist in the identification and to prescribe pest control measures. Sources for such assistance should be identified and located for quick reference when needed.

Some pest problems occur as a secondary effect, so their control becomes difficult or ineffective until the primary cause is identified and corrected. Such is the case, for example, in induced pest problems that gain a foothold because the crop is under element or environmental stress. Elemental deficiencies, water and temperature stresses can "set-up" a crop for the invasion by some ever-present, but not usually seen, pest. Older plant tissues become easy targets for some types of plant diseases and a desirable habitat for insects. A grower frequently finds his pest management program ineffective until his growing system is sufficiently well managed that elemental and environmental stresses are controlled. Therefore, it becomes important to determine the primary cause for a developing pest problem so that the correct action can be taken to regain control.

There are environmental and plant species associations that make hydroponic growing difficult. For example, in warm climates roots of tomato when in gravel or solution media, are easily attacked by the fungus, pythium (*Pythium aphanidermatum*). Most chemical and other techniques are normally ineffective for adequate control of this fungus disease, forcing the grower to select another crop. It is not unusual for the grower to have an excellent first crop free of disease infestation, only to find succeeding crops of the same species increasingly attacked by disease. Complete sterilization between crops of the entire system with steam or a chemical sterilant can eliminate the diseases, but the cost is high.

Disease control by discarding bags of media between crops is one reason this technique of soilless growing has gained in popularity over the older systems of gravel and sand culture which require sterilization between crops. Disposable plastic troughs are used in NFT systems to eliminate the need to sterilize the rooting channel. The opportunity to start off "fresh and clean" with a new crop has considerable advantage in terms of disease control.

Another very important means of pest control is the selection and use of resistant cultivars. Many of the more common plant diseases that used to plague growers are essentially eliminated by new cultivars that have been bred to specifically give disease resistance. New cultivars are introduced most every year and the grower must be aware of them, for they offer him the best means of disease control.

The most common disease problems affect plant roots. Some are extremely difficult to control. The various strains of pythium are a good example. Once this disease gains a foothold, it is almost impossible to control or eradicate. The grower is forced to select another crop species or terminate growing. Pythium is probably to most common and frequently occurring root disease problem, and in fact, it may be the most common of all diseases that can occur in hydroponic and soilless media systems. It is certainly the most talked about disease problem in the hydroponic literature. Unfortunately, there are no good control measures other than prevention.

The other common disease pests are the various fungi that inhabitat plant leaves. They vary in type and occurrence depending on the plant species and environmental conditions. These diseases are particularly severe when environmental conditions are warm and moist. Therefore, the essential control measures are devoted to keeping plant foilage dry and avoiding extremes in temperature. In some instances, keeping plant leaf surfaces covered with a recommended fungicide is required for control—to keep the disease from gaining a foothold. As was mentioned earlier, prevention is far more economical and effective than attempting to bring an infestation under control.

Bacterial and virus diseases are best controlled by selecting resistant cultivars. In a few instances, there are effective chemical control procedures. Some of these diseases are carried by insects so plant infection can be prevented by controlling the insect vector. Therefore, it is important to know the disease cycle and how it is carried from one plant to another, for by interruption of any one of the steps in the cycle, effective control can be obtained.

Insect control can be accomplished by several means. Insects are normally brought to the crop and it is usually their progeny that do the damage. Knowing something of the life-cycle of the insect pest can pinpoint the step easiest to interrupt. Therefore, as with most diseases, prevention is more effective than attempting to bring a damaging population under control. Knowing that an insect infestation might occur and the conditions suitable for it, the grower can then use the appropriate means for control even though the present population is insufficient to damage the crop. For example, white fly is a very common pesky insect which, if given a chance to gain a foothold, will damage a crop quickly and before control measures become effective. With this pest, active and more recently, passive control measures must be in place at all times. A fairly new and interesting way to control white fly is with yellow sticky boards placed strategically within the plant canopy. The fly is attracted by the yellow color and adheres to the sticky board upon contact.

One aspect of insect control, that varies to some degree as compared with disease control, is that some level of presence can be tolerated without the need for chemical action. This aspect does require some knowledge of insect and how to judge when control is or is not needed. In some instances, expert advice is required to make this decision.

Another aspect of growing which affects the extent of pest infestations relates to the density of the plant canopy. Dense plant canopies make an ideal habitat for many insects and diseases. The penetration of pest chemicals is commonly inhibited by the foilage, leaving areas of leaf surfaces uncovered. Temperature and humidity are often ideal for the regeneration and rapid growth of pests. By keeping the plant canopy open, accomplished by proper plant spacing, staking and pruning, providing air movement and reducing humidity, a less than ideal environment for these pests is created.

It is evident that an effective pest control program includes many elements: selection of resistant cultivars; use of good sanitation and cultural practices; and chemical control. The best pest management program is based on prevention rather than control after infestation. It is equally based on a knowledge of common pests and their effective control measures. Most growers are not sufficiently expert on pest identification and control; therefore, the use of consultants to assist in developing an effective pest management program is important. It is knowing what to expect, what to do and how to do it that can keep pests out, or salvage a crop if a pest gets in.

In the United States and many other countries, the sale and use of pest chemicals is carefully regulated. Licenses are required to purchase and/or use most pest control chemicals. The label plays an essential role in providing both information on crops that are cleared for its use and application procedures. Those who violate these regulations and label clearances are subject to stiff penalties. The greatest concern arises in connection with food crops where residues left on the edible portion can be hazardous. Since the laws and label clearances are constantly changing, the grower needs to be sure that his use of particular pest chemical is legal. The best source for current information on pest chemical use is the Agricultural Cooperative Extension Service in the United States, and similar governmental agencies elsewhere.

Chapter XI: Diagnostic Procedures

Success with any growing system is based to a considerable degree on the ability of the grower to effectively evaluate and diagnose the condition of his crop at all times. This is particularly true for the soilless culture system grower and absolutely essential for the hydroponic grower, since most, if not all, of the essential elements for the plants are being supplied by means of a nutrient solution. Errors in preparing and using the nutrient solution will affect plant growth, sometimes within a matter of a few days. Some growers possess a unique ability to sense when things are not right and take the proper corrective steps before significant crop damage is done. But most must rely on more obvious and objective measures to assist them in determining how their growing system is working and how their plants are responding to their management. In the latter case, there is no substitute for systematic observation and testing. In order to become a good diagnostician, time and experience are necessary.

Laboratory testing and diagnostic services are readily available in most areas. The grower should become familiar with them, their fields of expertise and services provided. Although routine testing and observation are time consuming and sometimes costly, the results can more than cover the costs in terms of a save crop and superior quality production. The grower should get into the habit of routinely analysing the growing media and crop, and carefully following recommended procedures to avoid yield reductions and crop losses.

A. PLANT ANALYSIS

As was discussed earlier (see Chapter IV), it is usually necessary to use diagnostic procedures to monitor the elemental content of the plant in order to ensure that all of the essential elements are being supplied in sufficient quantity to satisfy the crop requirement. This may be done on a regular routine of sampling and analysis, or in the hands of a knowledgeable grower when a suspected insufficiency seems to be developing. The usual procedure is called PLANT (or by some LEAF) ANALYSIS. A specific plant part is taken from a number of plants and submitted to a laboratory for analysis and evaluation.

Plant (leaf) analysis has heretofore largely been thought of as a diagnostic device, while its usefulness for monitoring has only recently been suggested and practiced. This latter role is probably most useful to the grower and is particularly valuable for those using any one of the soilless growing systems.

The objective for using plant (leaf) analysis, as a part of the growing routine, is to determine if the nutrient solution management technique is providing all the essential elements in their proper ratio and concentration, and so warn of possible elemental stress before an insufficiency or toxicity actually occurs. This procedure of routine sampling and analysis is frequently referred to as TRACKING. It is done to provide the information needed to establish the proper nutrient solution management procedures required to ensure that all of the essential element levels are within the sufficiency range for the crop being grown. It is well worth the time and expense to develop a track of elemental sufficiency, as shown in Figure 26, that can be used to firmly establish the proper nutrient solution management system for future use.

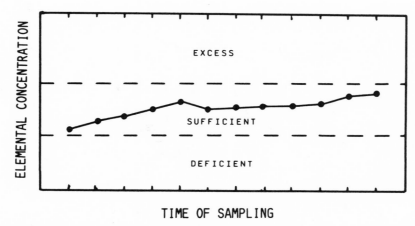

Figure 26. Essential element tracking as a technique for maintaining sufficiency.

The diagnostic role for plant (leaf) analysis is equally important. A grower, faced with a suspected essential element deficiency or imbalance, should verify the suspected insufficiency by means of plant (leaf) analysis. Many symptoms of elemental stress are quite similar and can fool the best trained. In addition, the stress may be due to the relationship between elements, and so require more than just a simple change in the nutrient solution formula to correct. Without an analysis, an incorrect change may be made which could further aggravate the problem.

Since a plant (leaf) analysis requires the use of a competent laboratory, contact with the laboratory should be made before samples are collected. The laboratory will provide sampling and submission procedures that are important to follow. One of the common sampling procedures is given in Table 18. If no specific sampling procedures are provided for a particular plant or the time period is not specifically provided, the "rule of thumb" for sampling is to collect recently mature leaves below the growing tip. This sampling procedure should be followed if the plants are being monitored in order to develop a track of their elemental content.

For diagnostic testing, when visual symptoms of plant stress are evident, it is advisable to take similar plant tissues from both affected and normal plants. In this way a comparison of difference is made which can be far more helpful than just an analysis of the stressed plants alone.

Plants which are diseased, insect or mechanically damaged should not be selected for sampling. Dead plant tissue should not be included in the selected sample. Tissue that is dusty or coated with chemicals should be avoided or if sampled, adequately washed as instructed in Table 19. In other words, great care should be used when selecting and sampling plants to be sampled and equal care taken in selecting the proper plant part.

Once the tissues have been collected, it is best to air dry them before sending them to the laboratory for analysis. This will keep them from rotting while in transit. Most laboratories can provide analyses for the majority of the essential elements and should be asked to make an evaluation of the analysis results based on the information submitted with the sample. Examples of interpretative plant analysis information is given in Table 20.

In order to conduct a complete plant (leaf) analysis, samples must be submitted to a laboratory equipped to do all the analytical work. On site tissue tests, however, can be made using tissue testing kits for the elements:

nitrogen as nitrate (NO_3^-),
phosphorus as phosphate (PO_4^{---}),
potassium (K^+), and
iron (Fe^{+++}).

TABLE 18. TYPICAL PLANT TISSUE SAMPLING PROCEDURES FOR CROPS FOR PLANT ANALYSIS EVALUATION

Crop	Stage of growth	Plant part	Number of plants to sample
Cucumber	Just prior to initial bloom and fruit set	Upper fully expanded leaves	10–15
Tomato	Prior to or during fruit set	*Young Plants:* leaves adjacent to 2nd and 3rd clusters	10–15
		Older Plants: leaves from 4th to 6th clusters	10–15

General Recommendations:
1. The best time to sample is during the mid-season of the crop; or when a suspected insufficiency occurs, at the initial signs of the difficulty. Samples taken late in the growth cycle of the plant are difficult to interpret in a plant analysis evaluation.
2. The General Rule of Thumb for sampling is to take upper mature leaves, leaves that are fully expanded, avoiding leaves that are diseased, mechanically or insect damaged, and those relatively free from dust and chemical contamination. Normally petioles are to be removed or not collected as a part of the sample.
3. When there is a visual suspected elemental insufficiency, leaf tissue samples should be taken from both affected as well as normal or near normal plants inorder to supply the analyzing laboratory typical samples representing the range of plant appearance.
4. Whole plant tops are not normally recommended as the sample unless the only sample available. Plants under a long period of stress are not suitable for sampling for plant analysis evaluation.

TABLE 19. WASHING PROCEDURE FOR REMOVING SOIL, DUST, CHEMICALS AND OTHER SURFACE ADHERING SUBSTANCES FROM LEAF TISSUE PRIOR TO ELEMENTAL ANALYSIS

1. Prepare a 0.2% Detergent Solution.
2. Place the leaf into the solution and lightly rub the surface with the fingers. Do not keep the leaf in the detergent solution more than 10 to 15 seconds.
3. Remove from the detergent solution and wash quickly in flowing pure water.
4. Remove excess water by shaking virgorously.
5. The leaf tissue is ready for drying.

Smooth surfaced leaves and tissues can be easily washed in this manner. Leaves that are rough or have pubescence surfaces are difficult, if not impossible to wash clean. Do not apply heavy pressure when rubbing the surface during the washing procedure.

TABLE 20. INTERPRETATION OF PLANT ANALYSES FOR SEVERAL CROPS

| Element | | *Tomato*[1] | | *Cucumber*[2] |
		prior to fruiting	During fruiting	During growing season
		.... %		
Nitrogen	(N)	4.00–5.00	3.50–4.00	3.75–5.00
Phosphorus	(P)	0.50–0.80	0.50–0.80	0.40–0.80
Potassium	(K)	3.50–4.50	3.00–4.50	4.00–6.00
Calcium	(Ca)	0.90–1.80	1.00–2.00	1.00–2.00
Magnesium	(Mg)	0.50–0.75	0.50–1.00	0.50–1.00
		.... ppm		
Boron	(B)	35–60	35–60	40–60
Copper	(Cu)	8–20	8–20	5–10
Iron	(Fe)	50–300	50–300	60–250
Manganese	(Mn)	50–200	50–200	50–200
Zinc	(Zn)	25–100	25–100	25–75

1. Prior to Fruiting Sampling: leaves adjacent to 2nd and 3rd clusters.
   During Fruiting Sampling: leaves from 4th to 6th clusters.
2. Seasonal Sampling: upper fully expanded leaves.

These "quick tests," as they are frequently referred to, can be useful in certain circumstances, but they are not adequate substitutes for the laboratory conducted plant (leaf) analysis. Although the test procedures themselves may be easy, the difficulty comes in interpreting the results. It takes considerable skill and practice to be able to use tissue test results effectively.

It is common practice to focus on single element deficiencies when dealing with nutritional problems in plants. Since intensive plant production is the usual objective in soilless growing systems, equal attention should be given to excesses and imbalances among all the elements. This is particularly important with hydroponic systems where nutrient solution management is critical to success. Careful monitoring of the nutrient solution as well as the plants themselves should be the normal practice.

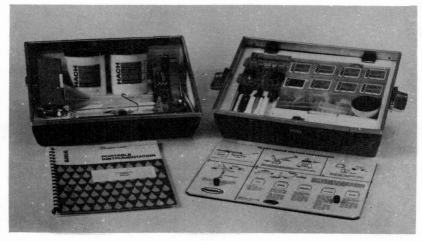

HACH Chemical Company plant analysis kit.
HACH Chemical Company, P.O. Box 389, Loveland, Colorado 80539.

As with water and nutrient solution analyses, the assay can be done by a commercial chemical testing laboratory, or by menas of special testing kits. One such kit suitable for conducting plant analyses is made by the HACH Chemical Company. Such kits can prove useful when quick test results are needed.

B. ELEMENTAL ANALYSIS OF THE GROWTH MEDIUM

Elemental analysis of plant growth medium, whether soil or a soilless mix, is an important part of the total evaluation of the elemental status of the media-crop system. When coupled with a plant analysis, it allows the evaluator to determine what elemental stresses exist and how best to bring them under control. This analysis may be a comprehensive one, determining the concentration present in the growth medium by element, or a more general one, measuring the total soluble salt content or effluent from the medium or by extraction of an equilibrium solution. A comprehensive test is more valuable as a means of pinpointing possible elemental problems than just a determination of the conductivity of the effluent or an extracted solution.

A test of an inorganic growth medium, such as gravel or sand, measures as is done with soil, the accumulation of salts that will significantly affect the elemental composition of the nutrient solution being circulated through it (see pages 50–54). The test procedures recommended are given in Table 21. It may be possible to alter the nutrient solution composition sufficiently to utilize the accumulated elements or begin to make adjustments in the nutrient solution formula with the idea of reducing the rate of accumulation while partially utilizing those elements already a part of the medium.

TABLE 21. ELEMENTAL ANALYSIS OF SAND AND GRAVEL ROOTING MEDIA

Reagent:

Mehlich No. 2 Extractant
> Add to a 1-liter flask about 750 ml of pure water, 11.5 ml glacial acetic acid, 10.7 g ammonium chloride (NH_4Cl), and 0.56 ammonium floride (NH_4F). Dissolve, add 1 ml conc. hydrochloric acid (HCl) and make up to volume with pure water.

Procedure:

1. Measure 10 cc of the media into a 250-ml Erlenmeyer flask.
2. Add 100 ml of Mehlich No. 2 Extractant.
3. Shake for 5 minutes.
4. Filter and save the filtrate.
5. Analyze the filtrate for its phosphorus (P), potassium (K), calcium (Ca) and magnesium (Mg) content. The HACH Water Analysis Kit is adequate to conduct this analysis, or the filtrate can be submitted to an analytical laboratory for the assay.

Interpretation:

> If the filtrate contains the same or greater concentration in parts per million as that in the nutrient solution for any of the tested elements, that contained in the media will have a significant affect on the supply and availability of that element to the plant. It may be possible to prepare the nutrient solution less that element and rely on the supply in the media to satisfy the plant requirement.

TABLE 22. SATURATION EXTRACT METHOD FOR ORGANIC ROOTING MEDIA

This procedure was developed at Michigan State University and has been routinely used for six years. It allows extraction of moist samples just as they come from greenhouses. Drying of samples is unnecessary and undesirable. Storage in greenhouse growth media in either the dry or moist state will influence the soluble nitrate-nitrogen and soluble salt levels. If samples will not be run within two hours of receipt, store them in a refrigerated area.

Equipment:

1. 600 ml plastic beaker.
2. Spatula.
3. Buchner funnel, 11 cm.
4. Filter paper (Whatman No. 1), 11 cm.
5. Vacuum flask, 500 ml.
6. Vacuum pump.
7. Vial, snap-cap 100 ml.

Procedure:

1. Fill a 600 ml beaker about 2/3 full with the growth medium. Gradually add distilled water while mixing until the sample is just saturated. At saturation the sample will flow slightly when the container is tipped and is easy to work with a spatula. After mixing, allow the sample to equilibrate for one hour and then recheck the criteria for saturation. The saturated sample should have no appreciable free water on the surface nor should it have stiffened. Adjust as necessary by addition of growth medium or distilled water. Then allow to equilibrate for an additional half hour.
2. Determine the pH of the saturated sample by carefully inserting the electrodes. Wiggle the electrodes gently to attain good solution contact.
3. Attach a Buchner funnel lined with filter paper to a vacuum flask. Apply a vacuum and transfer the saturated sample into the Buchner funnel. Work sample with a spatula and tap the funnel to eliminate entrapped air and insure good contact between the saturated sample and the filter. Continue vacuum, collecting the extract in the flask. No more than 15 minutes of vacuum should be required. Transfer the extract to the snap-cap vial. All subsequent analyses are done on the extracted solution.

Analysis

1. The saturation extract can be analyzed by a number of techniques for its content of nitrate (NO_3^-), ammonium (NH_4^+), phosphorus (P), potassium (K), calcium (Ca) and magnesium (Mg). HACH Chemical Water Analysis kit is adequate to conduct such analyses.

TABLE 23. GENERAL INFORMATION GUIDELINES FOR ORGANIC ROOTING MEDIA ANALYZED BY THE SATURATED EXTRACT METHOD

	Category				
Analysis	Low	Acceptable	Optimum	High	Very High
Soluble Salt, mmho/cm	0–.75	.75–2.0	2.0–3.5	3.5–5.0	5.0+
Nitrate-N, ppm	0–39	40–99	100–199	200–299	300+
Phosphorus, ppm	0–2	3–5	6–9	11–18	19+
Potassium, ppm	0–59	60–149	150–249	250–349	350+
Calcium, ppm	0–79	80–199	200+	—	—
Magnesium, ppm	0–29	30–69	70+	—	—

Additional details on the analysis procedure and interpretation can be obtained in the HANDBOOK ON REFERENCE METHODS FOR SOIL TESTING. 1980. Council on Soil Testing and Plant Analysis, Department of Horticulture, University of Georgia, Athens 30602.

The testing procedure for an organic growth medium is quite different as shown in Table 22. An aliquot of sample is brought into equilibrium with water, and the equilibrium solution removed and analysed. The ranges of concentration for the various elements, pH and soluble salts have been established by researchers at Michigan State University and are given in Table 23.

Although the testing procedures are quite different for each growing medium, the objective of the analysis is the same—to evaluate the elemental status of the medium for diagnostic purposes. The elements present in the growth medium serve as a major contributor toward meeting the crop requirement. Therefore, one objective for an analysis is to determine the level of each of the essential elements in the growing medium that will contribute toward satisfying the crop requirement.

The other purpose of medium analysis is to track preferential element accumulation by the medium. In systems where the bulk of the elemental requirement is supplied by a nutrient solution, growth medium analysis serves to determine accumulation rates so as to avoid imbalances and potential toxicities. In such cases, a conductivity measurement of the effluent from the medium, or an extraction of it, gives sufficient information. Many growers seem to be confused by the various means of measuring and expressing conductivity measurements. A brief discussion of conductivity is given in Table 11.

When the conductivity of effluent from the growth medium or an extract of it reaches a specified level (see Table 11), the growth medium should be leached with pure water to remove accumulated salts. In some systems, leaching of the growth medium on a regular schedule is part of the normal routine. Systems using regularly scheduled leaching should also be subjected to periodic analysis of the growth medium effluent to confirm that the regular leaching schedule is, in fact, doing the job intended.

TRACKING as was recommended for plant analysis (see Figure 26, page 89) can be used for following the elemental composition of the growth medium. The objective is similar, the following of the elemental concentration with time and making adjustments based on changing concentrations towards or beyond the sufficiency range. Periodic analysis becomes the means of regulating the input of the essential elements in order to prevent deficiencies or excesses from occurring.

C. NUTRIENT SOLUTION ANALYSIS

Elemental analysis of the nutrient solution is no different than periodically having the growth medium or effluent from it assayed. Such analyses are an important aspect of good management.

Errors in the preparation of the nutrient solution are not uncommon, making an analysis a check on the final elemental concentrations prior to use. Since the elemental composition of the nutrient solution can be altered considerably in CLOSED, recirculating systems, it is equally important to monitor the composition of the solution as frequently as practical. A record of the analysis results should be kept and a track developed to determine how the concentration of each element is changing. On the basis of such analyses, change schedules, replenishment needs, and crop utilization patterns can be determined. The track establishes the basis for adjustments in the composition of the nutrient solution to compensate for the "crop effect" not only in the current crop but for future crops as well.

In addition, periodic analysis allows the grower to adequately supplement the nutrient solution in order to maintain consistent elemental levels, ensuring good crop growth, as well as to extend the useful life of the nutrient solution. Significant economies can be gained by extending the life of the nutrient solution both in terms of water and chemical use.

Some remarkable developments in recent years have made routine analysis of the nutrient solution easier and cheaper. Laboratory analysis is recommended, although onsite analysis is possible with the use of kits and simple analytical devices. It is now also possible to continuously monitor the nutrient solution with devices, such as specific ion electrodes. Therefore, irrespective of the growing system in use, some type of analytical procedure should be used to monitor the composition of the nutrient solution as a normal routine.

As with the elemental analysis of the growth medium, the nutrient solution can be assayed on the basis of its individual elemental content or by measuring its total soluble salt content (see Table 11). Conductivity is frequently recommended as a means of determining elemental need in CLOSED, recirculating nutrient solution growing systems. This technique is useful if previous knowledge is available as to which elements are likely to change and by how much. It is far more desirable to do an analysis which quantifies each individual element and their ratios in the nutrient solution so that specific adjustments can be made to bring the nutrient solution back to its original composition.

As was discussed earlier (see page 57), it is highly desirable to maintain the composition of the nutrient solution at a constant level in CLOSED, recirculating growing systems. Continuous monitoring of the elemental concentrations in the nutrient solution provides the means of determining what additions are required to achieve constant composition. The results are improved crop performance, and better utilization of water and essential elements.

The analysis of the nutrient solution should include pH, and tests to determine the concentration of the major elements, nitrate (NO_3^--and ammonium (NH_4^+)-nitrogen (N), phosphorus (P), potassium (K), calcium (Ca), and magnesium (Mg). All of these determinations can be easily made on site using a water analysis kit (see page 36). Although similar kits are also available for some of the micronutrients, laboratory analysis will be necessary in most instances. However, concentration monitoring of the micronutrients is not as critical as for the major elements, unless there is suspicion of a micronutrient problem. For any diagnostic problem, laboratory analysis is always recommended, including all the essential elements—the major elements and micronutrients.

Chapter XII: Commercial Success and the Future

Most soilless culture systems WORK, that is the grower can construct the growing system, prepare and dispense the nutrient solution, and grow plants. However, there is a significant difference between a WORKING system and one that is COMMERCIALLY successful. Lack of universal commercial success to date has discouraged the use of some soilless growing systems for plant production. Most soilless culture systems require substantial capital investment due to the specialized equipment and control devices required. In addition, costs measures in terms of the time and skill required of the grower are considerable. The grower may, for example, spend as much time managing the nutrient solution as he does managing his crop. The current interest in bag culture, for example, is an attempt to simplify the growing system for the grower while maintaining some of the important aspects of the soilless culture technique.

High capital and operating costs help to explain why most types of soilless culture techniques are not more widely used. Most applications are limited to areas where other techniques of growing are not feasible or for crops having a high cash value. Soilless culture today is essentially limited to controlled environmental systems, rather than outdoor growing, such as the gardens established in the south Pacific during World War II and found in Florida shortly after the war years. Increased use of soilless growing basically hinges on the development of systems that will make the technique economically competitive with other growing systems.

More than just a WORKING system for soilless growing is needed, if capital investment and operating costs remain high. These increased costs must be offset by improved yield and crop quality so the grower can count on increased sales at better prices, and therefore, make a profit on his investment and labor input. Few, if any, of the current commercial soilless growing systems on the market today meet the criterion of cost effectiveness.

Soilless culture techniques possess an unique advantage which has yet to be fully exploited; that is, the capability of precisely controlling the rooting environment in terms of water and supply of the essential elements (as well as non-essential elements that may be beneficial to plants). Two systems that offer such an advantage are the hydroponic technique, aeroponics; and a soilless medium culture system based on the concept initially developed for staked tomato production on the sandy soils of west central Florida[32], a technique which provides precise water and essential element control. While one aeroponic system[31] is under development for commercial introduction, the technique has yet to be fully explored for adaptation to container type growing systems.

There is need for research to determine how best to constitute and manage the nutrient solution for maximum plant growth and development. There has been little significant development in this aspect of soilless culture since its first introduction as a commercial system for plant growing in the 1940s, when a California researcher named W. F. Gericke published a book on soilless gardening[33]. It was Dr. Gericke who coined the word HYDROPONICS, and his book sparked world-wide interest in the practical and commercial application for soilless growing. Numerous other books have been written on hydroponics and soilless growing, indicating the continuing interest in this technique. Today, we are still using Hoalgand nutrient solutions or slight modifications of them and

32. C.M. Geraldson. 1982. Tomato Production and the Associated Composition of the Hydroponic or Soil Solution. JOURNAL OF PLANT NUTRITION 5(8): 1091–1098.
33. W.F. Gericke. 1940. The Complete Guide to Soilless Gardening. Prentice-Hall, Inc., New York, New York.

TABLE 24. LIST OF ADVANTAGES AND DISADVANTAGES FOR THE HYDROPO-
NIC TECHNIQUE IN CROP PRODUCTION

Advantages:

1. Crops can be grown where no suitable soil exists or where the soil is contaminated with disease.
2. Labor for tilling the soil, cultivation, fumigation, watering, and other traditional practices are largely eliminated.
3. Maximum yields are possible, making the system economically feasible in high density and expensive land areas.
4. Conservation of water and nutrients is a feature of all systems. This can lead to a reduction in pollution of land and streams because valuable chemicals needn't be lost.
5. Soil-borne plant diseases are more readily eradicated in CLOSED systems which can be totally flooded with an eradicant.
6. More complete control of environment is generally a feature of the system, i.e., root environment, timely nutrient feeding or irrigation, and in greenhouse type operations, the light, temperature, humidity and composition of the air can be manipulated.
7. Water carrying high-soluble salts may be used if done with extreme care. If the soluble salts in the water supply is over 500 ppm (parts per million), an OPEN system of hydroponics may be used and care given to frequent leaching of the growing medium to reduce the salt accumulations.
8. The amateur horticulturist can adapt a hydroponic system to home and patio-type gardens even in high rise buildings. A hydroponic system can be clean, light weight and mechanized.

Disadvantages:

1. The original construction cost per acre is great.
2. Trained plantsmen must direct the growing operation. Knowledge of how plants grow and the principles of nutrition are important.
3. Introduced soil-borne diseases and nematodes may be quickly spread to all beds on the same nutrient tank of a CLOSED system.
4. Most available plant varieties have been developed for growth in soil and in the open. Development of varieties adapted to controlled growing conditions will require research and development.
5. The reaction of the plant to good or poor nutrition is unbelievably fast. The grower must observe his plants every day.

the same general methods for soilless growing as first introduced some 40 years ago! The only significant NEW development in hydroponics, as a growing system, came when Allen Cooper[7] introduced his NFT system in the mid 1970s (see pages 78–82).

In media culture, the use of organic in place of inorganic substrates, bag culture, such as the hanging bags of perlite, the subirrigation system using pine bark described earlier in this book (pages 72–73), and drip irrigation, are recent developments. They were born of economic necessity and out of the need to obtain some degree of control. The trend today in most hydroponic and soilless systems is to grow the plant in isolated containers, or in small beds and troughs. But, even with these changes in technique, they are in essence similar in technique as first described by Gericke, Hoagland and Arnon, and others, in the 1940s and 50s. In other words, we are still clinging to the basic concepts as set forth 40 years ago, even though there have been some changes in media type and container design.

Dr. Merle Jensen, a noted researcher in the application of the hydroponic technique for growing, presented an excellent review on "New Developments in Hydroponic Systems: Descriptions, Operating Characteristics, Evaluations," at the Second Annual Conference of the Hydroponic Society of America[34]. Dr. Jensen listed the advantages and disadvantages of "nutriculture"—his term for hydroponics (see Table 24) and concluded: "High yields of vegetables, fruits and flowers can be achieved when using any of the nutriculture systems. Most systems are extremely capital intensive therefore the author wishes to stress their use only on a hobby basis, rather than for commercial production in the U.S. New developments in energy alternatives and conservation, pest control, varieties and marketing will need to bring vast improvements in lowering operating costs before any or most of the systems discussed in this paper will become economical for production of most crops, especially greenhouse vegetable production."

34. Merle Jensen. 1981 New Developments in Hydroponic Systems: Descriptions, Operating Characteristics, Evaluations. pp 1–25. IN Proceedings Hydroponics: Where Is It Growing?, Hydroponic Society of America, Brentwood, California.

Chapter XIII: Summary

This book provides the user with a basic knowledge of plant nutrition and how this knowledge can be applied to the growing plants without soil. The objective has been to bring to the attention of the reader those factors essential for success when using a soilless growing system. It should be evident that soilless growing is not the panacea so often described, but requires of the user considerable skill. By balancing the supply of applied essential elements in order to avoid plant stress, the grower can achieve good plant growth which, in turn, results in high yield. Soilless growing provides the commercial grower with the ability to control the rooting environment in terms of water and elemental supply. But soilless growing systems demand of the grower full attention to the most minute detail because these systems can fail in one aspect or another so easily.

The various systems of plant growing in a rooting media offer the grower a variety of techniques, with both inorganic and organic rooting media from which to choose. CLOSED, recirculating nutrient solution systems using gravel or sand as the growing media are difficult to manage and are subject to endless problems. Growing in an organic media, such as sphagnum peatmoss, pine bark, etc., in some form of bag or bed culture, have been widely and successfully used. The essential plant elements are added to the medium either as a part of the growing mix or dripped into the growing medium as a constituent of the irrigation water. The use of perlite as a growing medium bathed with nutrient solution is proving to be a successful technique for some speciality uses.

There have been numerous nutrient solution formulas proposed, well in excess of 100, of which not more than one or two, are really basic. Those who experience elemental stress in their hydroponic growing system are simply failing to adequately manage the solution. They fail to recognize the relationship that exists between nutrient solution composition and method of utilization. The number of plants per volume of solution, change and replenishment schedules, as well as flow rate, influence the plant response to the composition of the nutrient solution. Unfortunately, most formulas do not give the required use information to guide the grower. One of the objectives of this book has been to provide at least some degree of guidance based on past and current experiences and research.

There is good evidence that unique relationships exist among and between the elements in the nutrient solution. As long as these relationships are maintained within certain bounds, the plant's elemental requirement will be satisfied. It is when these elemental ratios in the nutrient solution move outside the desired ratio range that plant stress occurs. The IDEAL nutrient solution is one in which the composition is maintained during its use so that the plant SEES only one constant concentration of elements in the solution. This ideal obviously points to the continuous supplementation of the nutrient solution in CLOSED soilless growing systems which recirculate the nutrient solution by adding back with each use those elements removed by plant absorption. Therefore, systems based on nutrient composition maintenance and balance, and combined with proper management (plant/volume ratio and flow rate), are going to be more successful in providing for the plant's elemental requirement than those systems based on weekly replenishment and/or supplementation.

It is evident that most soilless growing systems (including the generally practiced systems of hydroponics) work; that is, nearly anyone can grow plants with them. It is when these systems must be used commercially, and so in an economically sound fashion, that difficulties arise. Soilless growing systems are considerably more difficult to manage than growing in soil. Soilless growing is very unforgiving of errors made by the grower.

The soilless system grower must learn to rely on a well designed and managed routine procedure of diagnosis and testing. All three of the major components in growing must be included in this routine of analysis—the plant, rooting media, and the nutrient solution. The grower needs to become familiar with the patterns of elemental usage, techniques for pest control and requirements to maintain a proper elemental plant composition, which only routine elemental tracking can provide him, if maximum plant growth, development and yield are to be achieved.

Hydroponics, which has caught the attention of many, is only one type of soilless growing. It has the distinct advantage, when compared to other soilless growing systems, that it can be done in the absence of a rooting medium and; therefore, eliminates one major factor requiring management. However, there is not yet a hydroponic system commercially available that has proven to be financially sound. The future of hydroponics, as a significant and viable growing technique, probably lies with the development of aeroponics, or some system based on the South Florida technique of subsurface-nutrient solution control[32].

The future of the hydroponic technique as it is conceived and practiced today is yet to be settled. Present techniques are not suitable for commercial application and the IDEAL hydroponic system has yet to be devised. Closed systems that recirculate the nutrient solution, with or without the use of the root supporting medium, are difficult to manage as has been discussed to a considerable degree in this book. It could be that recirculation must be replaced with some other type of nutrient solution management technique, unless better control of the composition of the nutrient solution can be achieved than is now possible with current systems.

There are certain areas of the world where hydroponics seems to be the only system that can be used to successfully grow food crops despite the high costs and management difficulties. The desert regions of the world come to mind as likely candidates[35,36].

There is considerable interest in what has been termed INDOOR farming[37], the growing of plants in controlled environments under artificial lights and precise atmospheric conditions. In such systems, the value of the product must be sufficient to cover the high cost of production. Some of these costs may be offset by using power and heat considered WASTE from electrical generating plants, pumping stations and other sources. One of the largest such operations is located at the Drax power plant in central England where tomatoes are being grown by the NFT technique in waste heated greenhouses.

Probably one of the most important current and future uses for soilless and hydroponic growing will be by the individual as a means of providing food for himself and his family. Home gardening has increased substantially throughout the world. In many urban areas, soil resources are limited, or in some cases non-existent. In such circumstances, some non-soil method of growing must be employed. Because of space limitations and other factors, the growing system will have to be relatively small in size, highly efficient and easy to operate. In general, most soilless and hydroponic systems have been either large units for the commercial production of food or systems designed for non-food plants, such as woody ornamentals or flowering plants. Therefore, this special application will require considerable research and development effort to devise the best system to meet the requirements found in the urban setting. Some of the current soilless grow-box systems (see pages 72–74) or the aeroponic hydroponic technique may be best suited to meet this special need.

35. C.N. Hodges and C.O. Hodge. 1971. An Integrated System for Providing Power, Water, Food for Desert Coasts. HORTSCIENCE 6: 30–31.
36. M.H. Jensen and M.A. Tern R. 1971. Use of Controlled Environments for Vegetable Production in Desert Regions of the World. HORTSCIENCE 6: 33–34.
37. Anonymous. 1979. The Concept of Indoor Farming. AMERICAN VEGETABLE GROWER 27(5): 32.

XIV: Appendices

ENGLISH AND EQUAL METRIC UNITS	
ENGLISH	**METRIC**
LENGTH	
1 inch	2.54 centimeters
1 foot	0.30 meters
VOLUME	
1 fluid ounce	29.5 milliliters
1 gallon	3.78 liters
WEIGHT	
1 ounce	28.35 grams
1 pound	453.6 grams
TEMPERATURE	
0° F	−17.8° C
32° F	0° C
68° F	20° C
100° F	37.8° C
WEIGHT/VOLUME	
1 ounce/7500 gallons	parts per million (milligrams/liter) (micrograms/milliliter)

A. GLOSSARY

These definitions are oriented primarily to the "jargon" of soilless media culture and hydroponic growing, although some apply broadly to all forms of plant growing, and the botanical and horticultural sciences.

ABSORPTIVE CAPACITY:
    A measure of the capacity of a substance used as a growing medium in soilless culture to take (absorb) into pores and cavities nutrient solution. The trapped solution is a potential future source of water and essential elements. The composition of the nutrient solution is unaffected by this absorption. (See ADSORPTIVE CAPACITY)

ACIDITY:
    Refers to the pH of the nutrient solution or growth media when the pH measures less than 7.0. An increasing hydrogen-ion concentration leads to increasing acidity as the pH decreases from 7.0. (See ALKALINITY)

ACTIVE ABSORPTION:
    Refers to the process of ion uptake by plant roots requiring the expenditure of energy. This process is controlled and specific as to the number and type of ion species absorbed. (See PASSIVE ABSORPTION)

ADSORPTIVE CAPACITY:
    A measure of the capacity of a substance used as a growing medium in soilless culture to selectively remove from the nutrient solution essential elements by either precipitation, complexing or ion exchange. Adsorbed elements may be released and therefore, available to plants at a later time. The adsorptive capacity of a substance will significantly affect the composition of the nutrient solution through time depending on the degree of adsorption or release. (See ABSORPTIVE CAPACITY)

AERATED STANDING NUTRIENT SOLUTION CULTURE:
    A method of growing plants hydroponically where the plant roots are suspended in a container of continuously aerated nutrient solution. The usual procedure is to maintain the volume of the solution by daily addition of water and to replace the nutrient solution periodically with a fresh batch.

AEROPONICS:
    A technique for growing plants hydroponically where the plant roots are suspended in a container and are either continuously or periodically bathed in a fine mist of nutrient solution.

ALKALINITY:
    Refers to the pH of the nutrient solution or growth media when the pH measures greater than 7.0. A decreasing hydrogen-ion concentration leads to increasing alkalinity as the pH increases from 7.0. (See ACIDITY)

ANION:
An ion in solution having a negative charge. When applied to the composition of the nutrient solution, it designates ions such as, BO_3^{--}, Cl^-, $H_2PO_4^-$, HPO_4^{--}, MoO^-, NO_3^-, and SO_4^{--}, which are common forms for these essential elements in solution. In chemical notation, the minus sign indicates the number of electrons the compound will give up. (See CATION)

ATMOSPHERIC DEMAND:
The capacity of air surrounding the plant to absorb moisture. This capacity of the air will influence the amount of water transpired by the plant through its exposed surfaces. Atmospheric demand varies with changing atmospheric conditions. It is greatest when air temperature and movement are high, and relative humidity is low. The reverse conditions exist when atmospheric demand is low.

AVAILABILITY:
A term used to indicate that an element is in a form and position suitable for plant root absorption.

BAG CULTURE:
A technique for growing plants in a bag of soilless media (such as mixtures of sphagum peatmoss, pine bark, vermiculite, perlite, etc.) into which a nutrient solution is applied periodically.

BENEFICIAL ELEMENTS:
Elements not essential for plants but when present in the nutrient solution at specific concentrations or present in a rooting media enhance plant growth.

BORON (B):
An essential element classed as a micronutrient. Boron exists in the nutrient solution as the borate anion, BO_3^{---} The primary chemical source is boric acid (H_3BO_3).

BUFFER CAPACITY:
The ability of the nutrient solution or growth media to resist a change in pH during the period of its use.

CALCIUM (Ca):
An essential element classed as a major element. Calcium exists in the nutrient solution as the calcium cation, Ca^{++}. Major chemical sources are calcium nitrate [$Ca(NO_3)_2$], calcium chloride ($CaCl_2$) and calcium sulfate ($CaSO_4$).

CARBON (C):
An essential element classed as a major element. Carbon is obtained from carbon dioxide CO_2 in the air being fixed in the process called PHOTOSYNTHESIS.

CATION:
An ion in solution having a positive charge. When applied to the composition of a nutrient solution, it designates ions such as, Ca^{++}, Cu^{++}, Fe^{+++}, H^+, K^+, Mg^{++}, Mn^{++}, NH_4^+ and Zn^{++}, which are common forms for these essential elements in solution. In chemical notation, the plus sign indicates the number of electrons the element will accept. (See ANION)

CHELATES:
A type of chemical compound in which a metallic atom [such as iron (Fe)] is firmly combined with a molecule by means of multiple chemical bonds. The term refers to the claw of a crab, illustrative of the way in which the atom is held.

CHLORINE (Cl):
An essential element classed as a micronutrient. Chlorine exists in the nutrient solution as the chloride anion, Cl^-. Since the chloride anion is everpresent in the environment, it is not specifically added to the nutrient solution.

CHLOROSIS:
A light green to yellow coloration of leaves or whole plants which usually indicates an essential element insufficiency or toxicity.

CLOSED HYDROPONIC SYSTEM:
Designates a recirculation system of nutrient solution flow. (See OPEN HYDROPONIC SYSTEM)

CONDUCTIVITY:
A measure of the electrical resistance of a nutrient solution, or effluent from a growing bed or pot, and used to determine the level of ions in solution. Conductivity may be expressed as SPECIFIC CONDUCTANCE as mohs (micro- or milli-) or as resistance in ohms. (See SPECIFIC CONDUCTANCE)

CONTINUOUS FLOW NUTRIENT SOLUTION CULTURE:
A method of soilless culture in which the plant roots are continuously bathed in a flowing stream of nutrient solution.

COPPER (Cu):
An essential element classed as a micronutrient. Copper exists in the nutrient solution as the cupric cation, Cu^{++}. The primary chemical source is copper sulfate ($CuSO_4 5H_2O$).

DEFICIENCY:
Describes the condition when an essential element is not in sufficient supply or proper form to adequately supply the plant, or not in sufficient concentration in the plant to meet the plant's physiological requirement. Plants usually grow poorly and show visual signs of abnormality in color and structure.

DIFFUSION:
The movement of an ion in solution at a high concentration to an area of lower concentration. Movement continues as long as the concentration gradient exists.

DRIP NUTRIENT SOLUTION CULTURE:
A method of soilless culture in which the nutrient solution is slowly applied as drops onto the rooting medium.

ESSENTIAL ELEMENTS:
Those elements that are necessary for higher plants to complete their life cycle. Also, refers to the requirements established for essentially by Arnon and Stout. (See Chapter IV)

FEEDING CYCLE:
The time period when the nutrient solution is circulated through the root growing medium in those systems where plant roots are only periodically exposed to the nutrient solution.

GRAVEL CULTURE:
A soilless culture technique where plants are grown in beds containing gravel which are periodically bathed in nutrient solution. The gravel serves as a root support system for the plants.

HYDROGEN (H):
An essential element classed as a major element. Hydrogen is obtained from water, being fixed in the process called PHOTOSYNTHESIS.

HYDROPONICS:
A word coined in the early 1930s by Dr. W.F. Gericke, a University of California researcher, to describe a soilless technique for growing plants. The word was derived from two Greek words, HYDRO, meaning water and PONOS, meaning labor-literally WORKING WATER. Hydroponics has been defined as the science of growing plants without the use of soil, but by use of an inert medium to which a nutrient solution containing all the essential elements needed by the plant for normal growth and successful completion of its life cycle is periodically added. In this text, hydroponics refers only to those systems of soilless growing that do not use a rooting medium.

INTERMITTENT FLOW NUTRIENT SOLUTION CULTURE:
A method of soilless culture in which the nutrient solution is only periodically brought into contact with plant roots.

ION:
An atom or group of atoms having either a positive or negative charge from having lost or gained one or more electrons. (See ANION and CATION)

ION-EXCHANGE:
A method of water purification in which water is passed through a resin bed to remove both cations and anions from the water. Ion-exchange also refers to the phenomenon of physical-chemical attraction between charged colloidal substances with cations and anions. Ions of the essential elements can be removed from or released into the nutrient solution by ion-exchange characteristics of sphagnum peatmoss, pine bark, vermiculite, and clay colloids adhering to sand and gravel particles.

IRON (Fe):
An essential element classed as a micronutrient. Iron exists in the nutrient solution as either the ferrous, Fe^{++}, or ferric, Fe^{+++}, cation. The major chemical sources are iron tartrate, iron citrate and the chelate form, FeEDTA.

LEAF ANALYSIS:
A method of determining the total elemental content of a leaf and relating this concentration to the well-being of the plant in terms of its elemental composition. (See PLANT ANALYSIS)

MAGNESIUM (Mg):
An essential element classed as a major element. Magnesium exists in the nutrient solution as a cation, Mg^{++}. The primary chemical source is magnesium sulfate $(MgSO_4 7H_7O)$.

MAJOR ESSENTIAL ELEMENTS:
The 9 essential elements found in relatively large concentrations in plant tissues. These elements are: calcium (Ca), carbon (C), hydrogen (H), oxygen (O), magnesium (Mg), nitrogen (N), phosphorus (P), potassium (K) and sulfur (S).

MANGANESE (Mn):
An essential element classed as a micronutrient. Manganese exists in the nutrient solution as the manganous cation, Mn^{++}. The primary chemical source is manganese sulfate $(MnSO_4)$.

MASS FLOW:
The movement of ions as a result of the flow of water, the ions being carried in the moving water.

MICRONUTRIENTS:
The 7 essential elements found in relatively small concentrations in plant tissue. These elements are: boron (B), chlorine (Cl), copper (Cu), iron (Fe), manganese (Mn), molybdenum (Mo) and zinc (Zn).

MINERAL NUTRITION:
The study of the essential elements as they relate to the growth and well-being of plants.

MIST NUTRIENT SOLUTION CULTURE:
See AEROPONICS.

MOLYBDENUM (Mo):
An essential element classed as a micronutrient. Molybdenum exists in the nutrient solution as the molybdate anion, Mo^-. The primary chemical source is ammonium molybdate $[(NH_4)_6MO_7O_{24}4H_2O]$.

NECROSIS:
The dead tissue on plant leaves and stems which result from poor nutrition, disease damage, overheating, etc.

NITROGEN (N):
An essential element classed as a major element. Nitrogen is found in the nutrient solution as either the nitrate anion, NO_3^-, or the ammonium cation, NH_4^+. The primary chemical sources are ammonium nitrate (NH_4NO_3), potassium or calcium nitrate $[KNO_3, Ca(NO_3)_2]$ ammonium sulfate $[(NH_4)_2SO_4]$ and ammonium mono- or di-hydrogen phosphate $[(NH_4)_2HPO_4, NH_4H_2PO_4]$.

NUTRIENT FILM TECHNIQUE (NFT):
A technique for growing plants hydroponically in which the plant roots are suspended in a slow moving stream of nutrient solution. The technique was developed by Dr. Allen Cooper. (See pages 78–82)

NUTRIENT SOLUTION:
A water solution that contains one or more of the essential elements in suitable form and concentration for absorption by plant roots.

OPEN HYDROPONIC SYSTEM:
Designates an one-way passage of the nutrient solution through the rooting media or trough. After this single passage, the solution is dumped. (See CLOSED HYDROPONIC SYSTEM)

OSMOTIC PRESSURE:
Force exerted by substances dissolved in water which affects water movement into and out of plant cells. The salts dissolved in nutrient solutions exert some degree of force which can restrict water movement into plant root cells or extract water from them.

OXYGEN (O):
An essential element classed as a major element. Oxygen is obtained from carbon dioxide (CO_2) in the air, being fixed in the process called PHOTOSYNTHESIS.

PASSIVE ABSORPTION:
The movement of ions into plant roots carried along with water being absorbed by roots. (See ACTIVE ABSORPTION)

pH;
   The negative logarithm to the base 10 of the H-ion concentration.

$$pH = \log_{10} \frac{1}{[H^+]}$$

   pH being logarithmic, the H-ion concentration in solution increases 10 times when the pH is lowered one unit. The pH of the nutrient solution and rooting media will significantly affect the availability and utilization of the essential elements.

PHOSPHORUS (P):
   An essential element classed as a major element. Phosphorus exists in the nutrient solution as an anion, either as $H_2PO_4^-$ or HPO_4^{--}, depending on the pH. The primary chemical sources being ammonium or potassium mono—or di-hydrogen phosphate [$(NH_4)_2HPO_4$, K_2HPO_4, $NH_4H_2PO_4$, KH_2PO_4] and phosphoric acid (H_3PO_4)

PHOTOSYNTHESIS:
   The process by which chloroplasts in the presence of light split water (H_2O) and combine with carbon dioxide (CO_2) to form simple carbohydrates and release oxygen (O_2).

$$CO_2 + H_2O \xrightarrow[\text{in light}]{\text{chloroplasts}} CH_xO + O_2$$

PLANT ANALYSIS:
   A method of determining the total elemental content of the whole plant or one of its parts, and then relating the concentration found to the well-being of the plant in terms of its elemental requirement. (See LEAF ANALYSIS)

PLANT NUTRIENTS:
   Those elements that are essential to plants. (see MAJOR ESSENTIAL ELEMENTS and MICRONUTRIENTS)

PLANT NUTRITION:
   The study of the effects of the essential as well as other elements on the growth and well-being of plants.

PLANT REQUIREMENT:
   That quantity of an essential element needed for the normal growth and development of the plant without inducing stress from a deficiency or an excess.

POTASSIUM (K):
   An essential element classed as a major element. Potassium exists in the nutrient solution as a cation, K^+. The primary chemical sources are potassium chloride (KCl) and potassium sulfate (K_2SO_4).

REVERSE OSMOSIS:
A method of water purification in which ions are removed from the water by an electrical potential placed on either side of a membrane which acts to extract ions from a passing stream of water.

SALT INDEX:
A relative measure of the osmotic pressure of a solution of a fertilizer material in relation to an equivalent concentration of sodium nitrate ($NaNO_3$) whose SALT INDEX is set at 100. (See Table 10)

SAND CULTURE:
A soilless culture technique where plants are grown in beds containing sand which are periodically bathed in nutrient solution.

SCORCH:
Burned leaf margins. This visual symptom is typical of potassium (K) deficiency or chloride (Cl) excess.

SECONDARY ELEMENTS:
Now obsolete term used to classify 3 of the major essential elements, calcium (Ca), magnesium (Mg) and sulfur (S).

SOLUBLE SALTS:
A measure of the concentration of ions in water (or nutrient solution) used to determine the quality of the water or solution, measured in terms of its electrical conductivity. (See SPECIFIC CONDUCTANCE)

SPECIFIC CONDUCTANCE:
Specific conductance is the reciprocal of the electrical resistance of a solution measured using a standard cell and is expressed as mhos per cm at 25°C:

$$\text{Specific Conductance} = \frac{\theta}{R}$$

where θ is the cell constant and R is the resistance in ohms. Normally, the value is expressed as either micro- or milli-mhos. (See CONDUCTIVITY)

SUFFICIENCY:
The adequate supply of an essential element to the plant. Also, an adequate concentration of essential element in the plant to satisfy the plant's physiological requirement. The plant in such a condition will look normal in appearance, be healthy and capable of high production.

SULFUR:
An essential element classed as a major element. Sulfur exists in the nutrient solution as the sulfate (SO_4^{--}) anion. The primary chemical sources are K, Mg and NH_4 sulfates [K_2SO_4, $MgSO_4 7H_2O$ and $(NH_4)_2SO_4$, respectively].

SUMP:
The reservoir for storage of the nutrient solution in CLOSED, recirculating soilless culture systems.

TISSUE TESTING:
A method for determining the concentration of the soluble form of an element in the plant by analyzing sap that has been physically extracted from a particular plant part, usually from stems or pertioles. Tests are usually limited to the determination of nitrate (NO_3), phosphate (PO_4), potassium (K), and iron (Fe). Tissue tests are normally performed using simple analysis kits, with the elemental concentration found being related to the well-being of the sampled plant.

TOXICITY:
The condition in which an element is sufficiently in excess in the rooting media, nutrient solution or plant to be detrimental to the plant's normal growth and development.

TRACE ELEMENT:
Once in common use to designate those essential elements that are currently referred to as MICRONUTRIENTS. Trace element designates those elements found in plants at low concentration levels, usually at a few to less than 1 part per million of the dry weight.

TRACKING:
A technique of following through time the essential element content of the rooting media or plant by frequent analyses.

VALENCE:
The combining capacity of atoms or groups of atoms. For example, potassium (K^+) and ammonium (NH_4^+) are monovalent, while calcium (Ca^{++}) and magnesium (Mg^{++}) are divalent. Some elements may have more than one valance state, such as iron which can be either divalent, Fe^{++}, or trivalent, Fe^{+++}. This change from one valance state to another envolves the transfer of an electron.

ZINC (Zn):
An essential element classed as a micronutrient. Zinc exists in the nutrient solution as the cation, Zn^{++}. The primary chemical source is zinc sulfate ($ZnSO_47H_2O$).

B. TYPICAL VISUAL SYMPTOMS OF DEFICIENCY AND EXCESS FOR THE ESSENTIAL ELEMENTS FOR PLANTS

Element	Deficiency symptoms	Excess
Nitrogen (N)	General chlorosis or yellowing of the leaf tissue beginning with the older tissue. When severe the older tissue will turn brown while the younger tissue will be light green to yellow in appearance. Plants will look spindly, plant growth will become slowed and stop. Mature fruit will develop deep color.	Leaves dark green in color and foliage appearing lush and thick in appearance. Stems and main stalk lack strength, bending easily under weight of plant tops. Fruit development will be poor. Fruit will lack good color. *Ammonium Toxicity:* The plant may be chlorotic with lesions appearing on the leaves and stems. Plant growth will be stunted, the leaves may have a "cupped" appearance, and vascular tissue may begin to deteriorate resulting in wilting on high atmospheric demand days.
Phosphorus (P)	Dark green or a blue-green color develops which may turn to a purpling of the older leaf tissue, especially along the veins. When severe, the plants will becomed stunted and stop growing.	Excess P in plants results in deficiencies of the micronutrients, particularly zinc. Plants will be slow growing although otherwise looking fairly normal.
Calcium (Ca)	The younger tissue stops growing and may eventually die. The margins of the leaves may become chlorotic and turn brown. The fruit will develop "blossom-end rot," the development of black looking tissue at the blossom end. Root growth is severely reduced and readily susceptible to infection by bacteria and fungi.	Calcium is not considered a toxic element to plants but when in excess can affect the proper balance that is necessary with potassium and magnesium to maintain good growth. Plants may show symptoms of either potassium or magnesium deficiency, magnesium deficiency being the first to appear.
Potassium (K)	The plants will appear dark green or blue-green in color, similar to phosphorus deficiency symptoms, initially, and then dead or dying spots will appear on the leaves or along the leaf margins, giving the leaves a scorched appearance. Plants will become stunted when the deficiency is severe.	The appearance of potassium excess is that of either calcium or magnesium deficiency, magnesium being the more likely one to appear. Excess potassium causes an imbalance to occur.
Magnesium (Mg)	Deficiency symptoms appear on the older plant tissue as a marginal chlorosis and when severe, sections of the leaves will turn brown and die. There may be a relationship between magnesium deficiency and susceptibility to fungus diseases making the plant more liable to infection.	Excess magnesium may induce a potassium and/or calcium deficiency, depending on how the imbalance develops among these three cations. Visual symptoms may not appear although the plant may be growing poorly.

Element	Deficiency symptoms	Excess
Sulphur (S)	Symptoms of sulphur deficiency are not too dissimilar from nitrogen deficiency with plants appearing light green to pale yellow in color, depending on the severity of the deficiency. Normally, the symptoms are more general over the entire plant rather than being more apparent on the older leaf tissue which is typical of nitrogen deficiency.	Visual symptoms are not likely to appear as an excess seldom occurs.
Boron (B)	Growing tips become stunted and die. Leaves will be distorted, stems rough and cracked, often with corky ridges or spots. Flowering is severely affected and fruit set poor. Roots will stop growing and are readily susceptible to bacterial and fungus infections.	Toxicity will severely affect growth by stunting plants. If the toxicity is severe, the plant will quickly die.
Chlorine (Cl)	Deficiencies are not likely to occur. Only under the most unusual conditions does a chlorine deficiency arise. Deficiency symptoms are a bronzing of the leaves, followed by chlorosis and necrosis.	Excesses are fairly difficult to produce but if occurring will result in the stunting of the plants and wilting on high atmospheric demand days. Excess can interefere with the uptake of nitrate (NO_3^-).
Copper (Cu)*	Leaves will become chlorotic or deep blue-green in color with margins rolled up. Young shoots often die back and fruiting stops. The plants may become severely stunted.	Excess levels will severly affect plant growth, roots will be affected first and the plants will eventually die.
Iron (Fe)	A general chlorosis of the new tissue appears, the veins initially remaining green but then turn chlorotic. When severe, plant growth is slowed and the plants become stunted.	Under reasonable conditions, iron excess or toxicity will not occur.
Manganese (Mn)*	The younger tissue is chlorotic with the veins remaining green. Necrotic spots or streaks will appear on the leaves and black specks on the stems and leaf petioles. When the deficiency is severe, the plants will be stunted and the new leaves mis-shapen.	Visual symptoms may not be very different from deficiency symptoms initially. Necrotic spots will quickly appear, the plants will be stunted and possibly show signs of iron or zinc deficiency. Root growth will be slow or stop entirely.

* These elements, frequently referred to as the heavy metals, can be quite toxic to plants at elevated levels in the nutrient solution, being particularly toxic when plants are growing in solution without a root supporting media to serve as a buffer. These elements may have a direct effect on the plant or may generate an imbalance with other elements, giving the visual appearance of a deficiency of the interacting element. Great care should be used to prevent excessive levels from occurring in the making and use of the nutrient solution, or as a result of their accumulation in the growing media.

Element	Deficiency symptoms	Excess
Molybdenum (Mo)	An interveinal chlorosis will appear giving a mottled appearance. Leaf margins will tend to curl and roll.	Under reasonable conditions, molybdenum excess or toxicity will not occur.
Zinc (Zn)*	New leaves will be stunted, giving the appearance of a "Rosette" caused by the failure of the plant cells to expand and develop normally. Leaves may become twisted and necrotic, and sometimes chlorotic. When deficiency is severe, the plants will be stunted and misshapen.	Excessive zinc may be more apparent due to its effect on iron and possibly manganese, inducing symptoms of deficiency for these elements. Plants will appear chlorotic and severely stunted.

C. SIX TECHNIQUES FOR PREPARING AND USING NUTRIENT SOLUTIONS FOR SPECIFIC CROP USES

1. NUTRIENT SOLUTION FORMULA FOR SOILLESS TOMATO PRODUCTION

Complete nutrient solution method

This method supplies all the essential elements in a dilute solution and has been widely adopted by the British Columbia greenhouse tomato industry (Formula 1A). A recent modification using phosphoric acid in place of diammonium phosphate appears to have merit when the pH of the water supply is above 7.3 (Formula 1B). As well as supplying phosphorus, this acid effectively reduces the pH to an optimum level for nutrient uptake and prevents precipitation problems. These formulas can be adjusted to provide nitrogen (N) at three levels, and at each N level they supply phosphorus (P) at 37 ppm (84 ppm P_2O_5) and potassium (K) at 208 ppm (252 ppm K_2O). Although the P and K requirements of the plants remain constant throughout all stages of growth, the amount of N required increases as the fruits begin to develop.

PREPARATION. Dissolve each fertilizer separately in hot water and add each in turn to the required amount of water with agitation. In Formula 1A if the final solution has a pH above 6.5 it may appear milky; it can be cleared by adding sulfuric acid (specific gravity 1.265), usually 50 to 100 mL per 1000 L of nutrient solution, to bring it into the desired pH range of 6.0–6.5. In Formula 1B add the phosphoric acid first to prevent possible fogging of the solution, add the other ingredients, and if the pH is below 5.5, adjust the solution with potassium hydroxide to bring the pH into the 5.5–6.5 range. CAUTION: NEVER add water to acid.

Fertilizer premix method

The fertilizer premix method is a simple alternative in which minor elements, calcium, and magnesium in the form of dolomitic lime, and superphosphate are mixed with the medium before transplanting. Only nitrogen and potassium, the remaining essential elements, are applied routinely throughout the season in a nutrient solution (Formula 2A). This method is advantageous where the water source is alkaline but the sawdust is acidic. In such a situation, with no acid addition, the nitrogen-potassium solution can be applied without any danger of precipitation, and yet it will become acidified to a satisfactory level in the root zone. For the spring crop, incorporate 2.4 kg of 19% superphosphate (0-19-0) and 4 kg of dolomitic lime per cubic metre of sawdust. Apply half the dolomitic lime as coarse grind (12 AG) and half as fine grind (65 AG). This mix gives immediate and long-term availability of nutrients, which reduces the danger of calcium and magnesium deficiencies.

When the water supply is alkaline, a nonchelated minor element solution should be premixed with the sawdust at the rate of 1 L of stock solution diluted with 40 L of water per cubic metre of sawdust. Alternatively, in neutral or acidic water, the minor elements can be applied at the same rate as in Formula 1A with the nitrogen-potassium solution without danger of loss through precipitation.

Formula 2B containing phosphoric acid can be used to reduce alkalinity of the solution, and the superphosphate can then be omitted from the premix.

PREPARATION. (a) Dilute solution. Add separately dissolved ingredients to the required amount of water with agitation. For Formula 2B add the required amount of phosphoric acid directly to the water in the tank. If the pH of the final nutrient solution is below 5.5, add pelleted potassium hydroxide to bring it into the pH range of 5.5–6.5.

(b) Concentrate solution for diluter application. Confirm the dilution ratio of the diluter and based on this ratio dissolve the ingredients in Formula 2A or 2B in sufficient water to produce 160 L of dilute solution. In Formula 2B, check the pH of the diluted solution and, if necessary, adjust with pelleted potassium hydroxide as for dilute solutions (see previous paragraph).

FORMULA 1A

Fertilizer ingredient	Amounts of fertilizer per 1000 L		
	126 ppm* N	168 ppm N	210 ppm N
		grams	
Potassium sulfate (0–0–50)	500	300	nil
OR			
Potassium chloride (0-0-60)	420	250	nil
Potassium nitrate (13-0-46)	nil	225	550
Magnesium sulfate	500	500	500
Diammonium phosphate (21-53-0)	160	160	160
Calcium nitrate (15.5-0-0)	600	680	680
		millilitres	
Minor element stock solution**	220	220	220

* Parts per million = grams of nitrogen (N) per 1000 L
** Saanichton minor element mixes are available commercially with iron in either chelated or citrate forms, and contain the following ingredients:

	Iron chelate mix	Iron citrate mix	Minor elements in final nutrient solution
		grams	
Iron	70.0 (10% iron)	42.0 (16.7% iron)	1.54 ppm Fe
Manganese sulfate	15.0	15.0	1.07 ppm Mn
Boric acid	12.0	12.0	0.46 ppm B
Zinc sulfate	2.2	2.2	0.11 ppm Zn
Copper sulfate	0.6	0.6	0.034 ppm Cu
Molybdic acid	0.2	0.2	0.023 ppm Mo
	100.0	72.0	

To prepare the minor element stock solution, dissolve 100 g of dry iron chelate mix in 1 L warm water and store in dark bottle. If iron citrate mix is used as preferred for the fertilizer premix method (see above), dissolve 72 g in 1 L boiling water and store in dark bottle.

FORMULA 1B

Fertilizer ingredient	Amounts of fertilizer per 1000 L		
	126 ppm N	168 ppm N	210 ppm N
	grams		
Potassium sulfate (0-0-50)	360	44	nil
OR			
Potassium chloride (0-0-60)	300	37	nil
Potassium nitrate (13-0-46)	160	500	550
Magnesium sulfate	500	500	500
Ammonium nitrate (34-0-0)	nil	nil	100
Calcium nitrate (15.5-0-0)	680	680	680
	millilitres		
Phosphoric acid (75%)*	100	100	100
Minor element stock solution**	220	220	220

* Technical grade 75% phosphoric acid with a specific gravity of 1.58 and a P_2O_5 content of 54% is commercially available in Canada.
** See footnote to Formula 1A.

FORMULA 2A

Fertilizer ingredient	Amounts of fertilizer per 1000 L		
	126 ppm N	168 ppm N	210 ppm N
	grams		
Potassium nitrate (13-0-46)	550	550	550
Ammonium nitrate (34-0-0)	160	280	410
	millilitres		
Minor element stock solution*	220	220	220

* See footnote to Formula 1A.

FORMULA 2B

Fertilizer ingredient	Amounts in growing medium per 1000 L		
	126 ppm N	168 ppm N	210 ppm N
	grams		
Potassium nitrate (13-0-46)	550	550	550
Ammonium nitrate (34-0-0)	160	280	410
	millilitres		
Phosphoric acid (75%)*	100	100	100
Minor element stock solution**	220	220	220

* See footnote to Formula 1B.
** See footnote to Formula 1A.

(Source: E.F. Mass and R.M. Adamson. 1980. Soilless Culture of Commercial Greenhouse Tomatoes. Agriculture Canada Publication 1460.)

2. FORMULA AND PREPARATION METHOD FOR MODIFIED HALF-STRENGTH HOAGLAND'S SOLUTION*

The nutrient solution for feeding plants is prepared from two liquid stock concentrates which must be stored in separate containers to avoid precipitates (fiberglass or plastic-lined tanks are recommended). The concentrates can be stored successfully, but should probably be made up in batches only large enough to supply requirements for a few weeks.

When nutrient solution is to be recirculated through gravel beds, sand beds, or used in a continuous flow solution culture, combine equal quantities of the two stock concentrates in a container or reservoir capable of holding the required volume for a 200:1 dilution, as follows:

Stock concentrate	50 Gallons	100 Gallons	1,000 Gallons
No. 1	1 quart	2 quarts	5 gallons
No. 2	1 quart	2 quarts	5 gallons

The two stock concentrates have been calculated for use with a 200:1 fertilizer proportioner. For proportioners with other feed ratios, it will be necessary to change the amounts of the compounds used to prepare the concentrates, i.e., for 1:100 proportioning divide all measurements by 2. More concentrated solutions than those described should not be attempted, since precipitates will form, taking some elements out of solutions.

Stock Concentrate No. 1

	Amt/50 gal water
Potassium nitrate (KNO_3)	21 lb
Potassium phosphate* (KH_2PO_4)	12 lb
Magnesium sulfate ($MgSO_4 \cdot 7H_2O$)	21 lb
Micronutrient concentrate (formula follows)	5 gal

Fill with water and mix thoroughly to dissolve all salts.

Stock Concentrate No. 2

	Amt/50 gal water
Calcium nitrate [$5Ca(NO_3)_2 \cdot NH_4NO_3 \cdot 10H_2O$]**	38 lb
Sequestrene 330 Fe^+	2 lb

Mix the iron chelate thoroughly in a small amount of water before adding to the calcium nitrate concentrate.

Micronutrient Concentrate

	Amt/5 gal water
Boric acid (H_3BO_3)	54 gm
Manganese sulfate ($MnSO_4 \cdot H_2O$)	28 gm
Zinc sulfate ($ZnSO_4 \cdot 7H_2O$)	4 gm
Copper sulfate ($CuSO_4 \cdot 5H_2O$)	1 gm
Molybdic acid ($MoO_3 \cdot 2H_2O$)	0.5 gm

Dissolve boric acid in boiling water. Add other salts to a 5-gallon container and mix thoroughly in about 3 gallons of water. Add dissolved boric acid, then fill to 5 gallons.

APPROXIMATE CONCENTRATION OF NUTRIENTS IN FINAL SOLUTION

	NO_3-N	H_2PO_4-P	K	Ca	Mg	SO_4-S	Fe	B	Mn	Zn	Cu	Mo
PPM	103	33	140	83	24	32	2.5	0.25	0.25	0.025	0.01	0.005
meq/1[††]	7.5	1	3.5	4	2	2						

*This is the monobasic form. In order to use the dibasic form (K_2HPO_4) the formula would have to be recalculated.

** Based on the use of commercial grade material.

† Sequestrene 330 Fe is manufactured by Geigy Chemical Company. Until alternate proprietary compounds have been investigated, this is the only material which can be recommended.

†† meq/1 = milliequivalent per liter.

(Source: Hunter Johnson, Jr. 1980 Hydroponics: A Guide to Soilless Culture Systems. Division of Agricultural Sciences, University of California, Leaflet 2947.)

3. JUTRAS' COMPLETE NUTRIENT SOLUTION #1

Ingredients	grams / liter of water	approximate level spoonfuls per gallon
(a)		
NH_4NO_3 (ammonium nitrate)	0.25	⅓ tsp.
KNO_3 (potassium nitrate)	0.25	⅓ tsp.
$Ca(NO_3)_2$ (calcium nitrate)	0.25	¼ tsp.
$CaSO_4$ (calcium sulfate)	0.15	½ tsp.
KCl (potassium chloride; muriate of potash)	0.25	⅓ tsp.
$MgSO_4$ (magnesium sulfate; epsom salt)	0.25	⅓ tsp.
KH_2PO_4 (potassium monobasic phosphate), is a source of phosphorous as well as a buffer (pH stabilizer). If EDTA chelate is used (see below), add immediately. If chelate is not used, add the KH_2PO_4 after 2 or 3 days to give plants a chance to pick up iron first.	0.30	½ tsp.
EDTA (chelate) (ethylenediamine tetraacetic acid. A chelate ties up reactive sites on micronutrients preventing their precipitation by reactions with phosphorus, especially).	0.12	¼ tsp.
(b) Prepare a separate micronutrient solution of the following, and add 1 ml of this micronutrient solution to each liter of the above solution (about 10 drops per quart):		
H_3BO_3 (boric acid), or	2.5	4 tsp.
$Na_2B_4O_7 \cdot 10H_2O$ (sodium borate; borax)	3.75	2 tsp.
$MnCl_2 \cdot 4H_2O$ (manganese chloride), or	1.50	1¼ tsp.
$MnSO_4 \cdot H_2O$ (manganous sulfate)	1.50	2 tsp.
$ZnCl_2$ (zinc chloride), or	0.20	¼ tsp.
$ZnSO_4 \cdot 7H_2O$ (zinc sulfate)	0.40	½ tsp.
$CuCl_2 \cdot 2H_2O$ (cupric chloride), or	0.20	¼ tsp.
$CuSO_4 \cdot 5H_2O$ (cupric sulfate)	0.20	¼ tsp.
$H_2MoO_4 \cdot H_2O$ (molybdic acid), or	0.05	pinch
$Na_2MoO_4 \cdot 2H_2O$ (sodium molybdate)	0.05	pinch

Remember, add only 1 ml of this micronutrient solution to each liter of the first solution.

(c) Prepare a third solution of an iron compound; use 0.5 gram of ferric sulfate, or ferric acetate, or ferric citrate, or ferric tartrate, or any other available iron salt including chelated iron, to 99.5 ml of water (1 pinch per quart). Then add 1 ml of this iron solution to each liter of solution a (about 10 drops per quart of solution a). Keep the solution stirred while extracting the 1 ml transfer sample to keep the iron suspended evenly throughout the solution. To save this solution for future use, be certain to enclose it in foil and store in a cool, dark place.

(d) Since the micronutrient-containing chemicals needed for solutions b and c are not as easily obtained (see section E), you may substitute 100 grams of seaweed (the wettable powder) per liter of water (about 6 measuring cupfuls per gallon of water), or use 1 liter of liquid seaweed with each liter of solution a (an equal amount of each solution mixed together) to provide the micronutrients.

(e) The pH of this solution should be around 4.5 after reparation; don't alter unless you wish to use the solution only as a fertilizer solution.

(Source: M.W. Jutras 1979 Nutrient Solutions for Plants. South Carolina Agricultural Experiment Station Cicular 182.)

4. NUTRIENT SOLUTION FORMULA FOR TOMATOES GROWN BY NFT

Starting Solution

Chemical	grams/100 liters	Element	ppm
$Ca(NO_3)_2 4H_2O$	84.2	N	100
$CaSO_4 2H_2O$	30.5	K	300
K_2SO_4	49.6	P	60
KH_2PO_4	26.8	Ca	215
$MgSO_4 7H_2O$	46.2	Mg	46
FeNaEDTA	6.55	S	150
$MnSO_4 4H_2O$	0.82	Fe	10
H_3BO_3	0.172	B	0.3
$NH_4Mo_7O_{24} 4H_2O$	0.005	Cu	0.1
$CuSO_4 5H_2O$	0.04	Zn	0.1
$ZnSO_4 7H_2O$	0.044	Mo	0.02

Topping Up Solution*

Chemical	grams/liter
K_2SO_4	66.8
$MgSO_4 7H_2O$	46.2
FeNaEDTA	6.55
$MnSO_4 4H_2O$	1.00
H_3BO_3	0.172
$(NH_4)_2Mo_7O_{24} 4H_2O$	0.005
$Ca(NO_3)_2 4H_2O$	84.2
90% H_3PO_4	12 ml/1

* dilute 1/100 for use

Plants are started with the STARTING SOLU-
TION and the make-up water consists of the
TOPPING UP SOLUTION.

(Source: G.C.S. Wilson. 1980. Effect of N:K Ratio in a Hydroponic Situation. pp 161–170. IN Symposium on Research on Recirculating Water Culture. ACTA HORTICULTURAE No. 98)

5. NUTRIENT SOLUTION FORMULA FOR GROWING CUCUMBERS HYDROPONICALLY

Major Element Formula

Chemical	Concentration (ppm)	for 5000 L	for 1000 gal.
(1) A. Potassium chloride (0-0-60)	210-K	2100 g	67 oz.
Magnesium sulphate	25-Mg	1250 g	40 oz.
B. Diammonium phosphate (21-53-0)	33-N 36-P	780 g	27 oz.
C. Calcium nitrate (15.5-0-0)	135-N 210-Ca	4360 g	140 oz.
(2) A. Potassium chloride (0-0-60)	117-K	1180 g	38 oz.
Potassium nitrate (13-0-44)	86-K 30-N	1180 g	38 oz.
Magnesium sulphate	25-Mg	1250 g	40 oz.
B. 75% phosphoric acid	33-P	450 ml	14.3 fl. oz.
C. Calcium nitrate (15.5-0-0)	135-N 210-Ca	4360 g	140 oz.

Formula (2) may be more satisfactory if the pH of the water supply is particularly alkaline.

Micronutrient Formula

Chemical	Concentration (ppm)	for 5000 L (grams)	for 1000 gal. (grams)
Iron chelate (10% Fe)	1.0	49.8	45
Manganese sulphate (28% Mn)	0.3	5.35	4.9
Borax (11.4% B)	0.7	30.5	27.8
Zinc sulphate (36% Zn)	0.1	1.38	1.26
Copper sulphate (25% Cu)	0.03	0.59	0.54
Molybdenum Trioxide (54% Mo)	0.05	0.46	0.42

Adjust pH to 6.0–6.5 as required

Use: For cucumbers use 530 mL/5000 L (17fl. oz./1000 gal.). It will be necessary to supplement the boron by adding an additional 15.5 g of borax per 5000 L (0.5 oz./1000 gal.).

(Source: Greenhouse Cucumber and Tomato Production Guide 1981 Ministry of Agriculture and Food, Province of British Columbia, Canada.)

6. NUTRIENT SOLUTION FORMULAS FOR CLOSED AND OPEN SYSTEMS

Salt — Fertilizer Grade Chemicals Analysis designed as % N-P-K	TOMATO — A Seedlings-First fruit set		TOMATO — B Fruit Set-Term. of Crop		CUCUMBER — C Seedlings-First fruit set		CUCUMBER — D Fruit Set-Term. of Crop	
	ppm	Grams per 1,000 liters	ppm	Grams per 1,000 liters	ppm	Grams per 1,000 liters	ppm	Grams per 1,000 liters
Magnesium Sulfate $MgSO_4 \cdot 7H_2O$ (Epsom salt grade)	Mg 50	500	Mg 50	500	Mg 50	500	Mg 50	500
Monopotassium Phosphate KH_2PO_4 (0-22.5-28.0)	K 77 P 62	270	K 77 P 62	270	K 77 P 62	270	K 77 P 62	270
Potassium Nitrate, KNO_3 (13.75-0-36.9)	K 77 N 28	200	K 77 N 28	200	K 77 N 28	200	K 77 N 28	200
*Potassium Sulfate K_2SO_4 (0-0-43.3)	K 45	100	K 45	100	—	—	—	—
Calcium Nitrate, $Ca(NO_3)_2$ (15.5-0-0)	N 85 Ca 122	500	N 116 Ca 165	680	N 116 Ca 165	680	N 232 Ca 330	1357
**Chelated Iron FE 330	Fe 2.5	25	Fe 2.5	25	Fe 2.5	25	Fe 2.5	25
***Micro-Nutrients	—	150ml.	—	150ml.	—	150ml.	—	150ml.

*The use of K_2SO_4 is optional.

**Up to 5 ppm of Iron may be needed if a calcareous growing medium is used.

***See micro-nutrient preparation table.

NOTE: In growing other vegetable crops use Solution C.
—Leafy vegetables—200 ppm N
—There are 454 g. per pound, 3785 ml. per gallon and 28.35 g. per ounce

MICRONUTRIENT FORMULA FOR CLOSED & OPEN SYSTEMS*

Salt	Element supplied	ppm of element	Grams of each micronutrient in the packet*
Boric Acid (H_3BO_3)	B	.44	7.50
Manganous Chloride ($MnCl_2 \cdot 4H_2O$)	Mn	.62	6.75
Cupric Chloride ($CuCl_2 \cdot 2H_2O$)	Cu	.05	0.37
Molybdenum Trioxide (MoO_3)	Mo	.03	0.15
Zinc Sulfate ($ZnSO_4 \cdot 7H_2O$)	Zn	.09	1.18

*One packet (15.95 grams) micronutrients + water to make 450 ml. micronutrient stock solution (heat to dissolve). Use 150 ml. for each 1,000 liters solution, 570 ml. for each 1,000 gallons (or 20 grams of micronutrient powder for each 1,000 gallons of solution.)

Index